THE WRECK OF THE AMSTERDAM

An eighteenth century rendering of the arms of the City of Amsterdam (Reproduced by courtesy of the City of Amsterdam)

The Wreck of the Amsterdam

PETER MARSDEN

Hutchinson

London Melbourne Sydney Auckland Johannesburg

Hutchinson & Co (Publishers) Ltd
An imprint of the Hutchinson Publishing Group
17–21 Conway Street, London W1P 6JD

Hutchinson Publishing Group (Australia) Pty Ltd
16–22 Church Street, Hawthorn, Melbourne, Victoria 3122

Hutchinson Group (NZ) Ltd
32–34 View Road, PO Box 40–086, Glenfield, Auckland 10

Hutchinson Group (SA) Pty Ltd
PO Box 337, Bergvlei 2012, South Africa

First published 1974
Second (revised) edition 1985
© Peter Marsden 1974 and 1985
© illustrations, unless otherwise acknowledged, Peter Marsden 1974 and 1985

Set in Monophoto Ehrhardt by Servis Filmsetting Ltd, Manchester
Printed and bound in Great Britain by
Anchor-Brendon Ltd, Tiptree, Essex

ISBN 0 09 160811 2

Dedication

To the two people, Vernon Leonard and Olaf Heyligers, without whose particularly substantial contribution to the *Amsterdam* project, the publication of a new edition of this book would not have been possible.

Typical of the excellent cooperation between our two countries in this project is the fact that, of the two people who have been outstanding in raising public consciousness of the unique value of the recovery of the *Amsterdam*, one is English and the other Dutch. Vernon Leonard, formerly Editor of the Dutch magazine *Holland Herald*, headed a most successful campaign in the 1970s to alert the people of the Netherlands to the importance of the ship to their maritime heritage, and Olaf Heyligers, CBE, member of the Board of the Amsterdam Foundation, who as Chairman of the Excavation Committee initiated the excavations of 1984 and 1985.

Contents

Illustrations

9

ILLUSTRATIONS

FIGURES IN TEXT

11

ILLUSTRATIONS

Foreword

In the summer of 1969 a group of amateur treasure hunters started digging away with high-powered mechanical excavators at the then more or less unknown wreck of the 18th century Dutch East Indiaman *Amsterdam*, which on her maiden voyage got caught in a heavy storm, lost her rudder and was beached near Hastings, on England's south coast.

Fortunately this vandalism was soon stopped, archaeologists and historians took over, and under the leadership of Peter Marsden from the Guildhall Museum – now the Museum of London – scientific research was started into the condition of the wreck, her history, the people who sailed in the ship and the possibility of eventually raising her and taking her home.

In 1974 Peter Marsden published a fascinating book about his findings, both in English and Dutch. It raised considerable interest and in the Netherlands a trust was founded – its English name: the Save the Amsterdam Foundation – which has as its object to raise the *Amsterdam* and take her back to her native city, whose name she bore, conserve her and put her on display.

To prepare the ground for this large operation, in order to acquire the necessary experience, information and publicity, an excavation of part of the lower gun deck was carried out by British and Dutch divers, conservators, etc, in the summer of 1984 under the leadership of Peter Marsden. The wealth of information then gained has led to this new and revised edition of his 1974 book, which, I'm sure, again will interest a large public.

The fact that we are today much nearer to raising the *Amsterdam* will – in no small amount – be due to Peter Marsden's tireless efforts to rescue this unique historical monument of 18th century seafaring.

Mr dr C.J.M.A. van Rooy
Chairman of the Save the Amsterdam Foundation

Introduction

At low tide on certain days each year the gnarled and blackened ribs of the wreck of a Dutch merchant ship, the East Indiaman *Amsterdam*, can be seen thrusting out like ancient teeth from the level shore near Hastings, on the south coast of England. They never fail to attract sightseers, who poke at the timbers as the sunlit waves lap gently on the glistening golden sand. As a result of intensive research, both by excavation on the site and by delving into 18th century Dutch and English archives, her fascinating story is now increasingly well known. The *Amsterdam* was abandoned by her Dutch owners as a total loss soon after her wreck in 1749, but as limited excavations in 1969 and 1970 proved, two-thirds of the ship's hull remains. This was confirmed in the investigation carried in 1984, and it is clear that, not only is her cargo substantially complete, but also that many personal possessions of her passengers and crew are still within the ship. The *Amsterdam* is an almost untouched storehouse of the life of the period, and forms one of the most historically valuable sites in European archaeology.

The natural home for the ship and her contents, when recovered and prepared for exhibition, is undoubtedly the city of *Amsterdam*, where she was built and whence she sailed on her disastrous maiden voyage almost two and a half centuries ago. This was my point of view as a specialist in historic shipwrecks, when I became responsible for the investigations undertaken on the site, right from the beginning in 1969. It was in that year that spare-time workmen constructing a nearby new sewer outfall, first called attention to the site, for they found hundreds of fine objects in excellent condition. Together with all those who have since given so freely of their time, skills and specialised knowledge to help with the project, I have always worked with the aim of one day seeing the ship return to the Netherlands, but the cost is undoubtedly astronomically high. It is, of course, undeniable that the project could be more economically carried out if her preservation was locally based. If in the end it proves to be too difficult to return the ship to the Netherlands, then it may be necessary to consider finding her a home in

Hastings. A large site at the rear of Hastings harbour is at present under development as a 'Shipwreck Heritage Centre' by the Nautical Museums Trust in connection with the remains of a number of fine ships which still survive in the area, notably the 17th century warship *Anne* which has interesting links with Pepys, and is already owned by the Trust. If need be there is room here for the *Amsterdam*. For, not only is it essential that she be preserved but, now that the site has to some extent been disturbed by the essential preliminaries to the planned full excavation, the work must be speedily completed to avoid further deterioration.

Those who have helped rediscover the story of the *Amsterdam*, both British and Dutch, are too numerous for all their names to be recorded here, but special thanks are due to the British Broadcasting Corporation and notably to Ray Sutcliffe, as also to Joop Reinboud of the Dutch television service KRO, who did much research among the Dutch East India Company's records and other sources in the Netherlands. I am very glad to be able to include in this volume as an appendix, the ship's paybook – giving details of all those aboard – which Joop discovered, and which is one of only a very few to have survived.

I am specially glad to be able to thank here Mr dr Charles van Rooy, Chairman of the Foundation for the Dutch East India Company ship *Amsterdam* (Stichting VOC Schip Amsterdam), and other members of its Board, both past and present. Particularly generous help was also given by John Manwaring Baines (formerly Curator of Hastings Museum), Bill and Ann St John Wilkes, Jeremy Green, Rex Cowan, Professor Charles Boxer, Jon Adams, the late Dr Simon Hart of the Amsterdam Municipal Archives, Jerzy Gawronski, Gerrit van der Heide, Stephen Challercombe (Director of Tourism of Hastings Borough Council), Pieter Yperdaan, the members of the Hastings Area Archaeological Research Grup, and Mr B. Slot of the Dutch State Archives (Rijksarchif). I should like to thank the various companies which have assisted the project with staff and equipment, particularly Itt Flygt, Hymac Ltd, and Smit Tak.

Finally, I am also grateful to my wife Fran, and my editor, Edith M. Horsley of Hutchinson, who read the draft text and did so much towards creating a more interesting and readable book.

I

Captain Willem Klump

As the carriage drew away from his typically narrow-fronted house overlooking the Prinsengracht canal, near the Anjeliersgracht, in Amsterdam, there would have been a surge of excitement beneath Willem Klump's sadness at leaving his family. It was October 1748 and, at thirty-three, he was taking over as only his second command, the *Amsterdam*, the latest new ship of the Dutch East India Company. It was something of an achievement, and the fact that she was an East Indiaman conjured up a vision of trade in exotic spices in Far Eastern waters, of strange people and rare sights, all to be encountered on the other side of the world. Even so, the parting with his wife, Margareta, must have been hard. It had been only four months since the birth of their latest child, a brother for their four-year-old daughter Elysabet. Both parents knew that baby Coenraad would be a walking, talking two-year-old when Klump returned from his voyage – if he did return.

Before arriving at the waterfront, Klump would almost certainly have called at East India House. This unpretentious building, not far from his own home, was in the heart of the city. Its simple frontage gave no hint that the Dutch East India Company was one of the greatest and most ambitious commercial trading organisations that the world had ever known, with its own army, navy and local and central government. Here, at the Amsterdam headquarters of the Verenigde Oost-Indische Compagnie – the name usually being abbreviated to VOC – Klump would collect his charts, navigation instruments, and sailing instructions for Batavia (modern Jakarta) in Java, before continuing his ride over the narrow, cobbled streets and the hump-backed bridges spanning the canals. His embarkation point was probably on the broad Y estuary, an inlet of the Zuyder Zee, close to the mouth of the River Amstel.

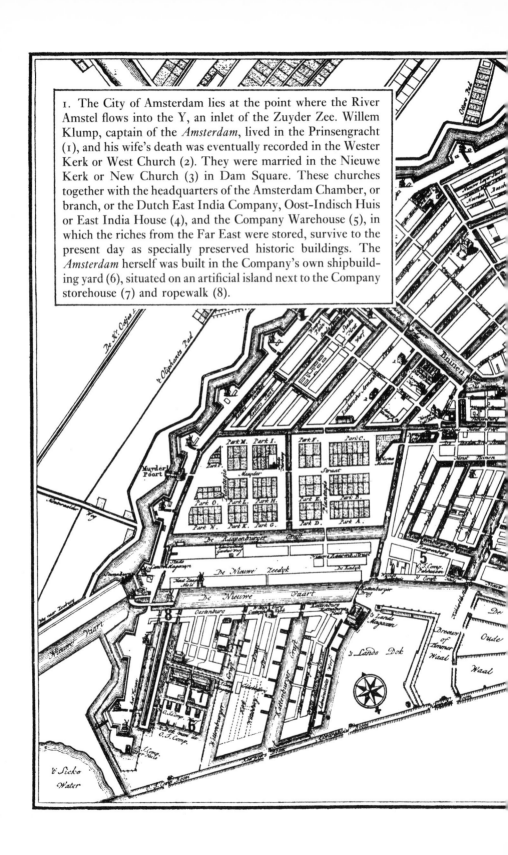

1. The City of Amsterdam lies at the point where the River Amstel flows into the Y, an inlet of the Zuyder Zee. Willem Klump, captain of the *Amsterdam*, lived in the Prinsengracht (1), and his wife's death was eventually recorded in the Wester Kerk or West Church (2). They were married in the Nieuwe Kerk or New Church (3) in Dam Square. These churches together with the headquarters of the Amsterdam Chamber, or branch, or the Dutch East India Company, Oost-Indisch Huis or East India House (4), and the Company Warehouse (5), in which the riches from the Far East were stored, survive to the present day as specially preserved historic buildings. The *Amsterdam* herself was built in the Company's own shipbuilding yard (6), situated on an artificial island next to the Company storehouse (7) and ropewalk (8).

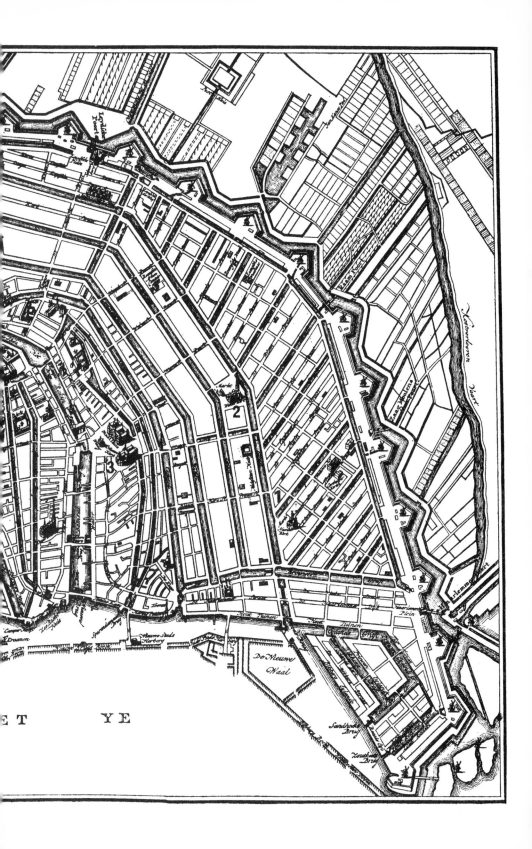

ET   YE

At this terminal the Company's major voyages began and ended. Alongside the quay a fleet of bluff-fronted ferry barges were moored, ready to take out the crew and passengers to the big ships, the 'ocean liners' of the eighteenth century. The autumn treasure fleet was now assembling off the Isle of Texel at the North Sea mouth of the Zuyder Zee, and was the largest and most important of the three VOC fleets which annually sailed to the Indies. This was the time of year when, as the days grew appreciably shorter at the end of October and the trees lining the canals turned to gold, the Amsterdam waterfront became alive with soldiers and sailors marching to embark. The quay by the Schreierstoren tower was known as 'the place of tears', for it was here that families parted as wives and sweethearts waved goodbye to their loved ones. Perhaps Margareta, in spite of her young children, also accompanied her husband as far as this.

As Klump ran an experienced eye over the men waiting to be crammed into the flat-bottomed ferries, there would have been many looking sullen and sickly. The crimps who entrapped men for service kept them in any miserable hovel or damp cellar in the city until they were actually engaged to man the ships of the VOC. The conditions in which the men were then held 'captive' were inhuman. An eyewitness reported that he had seen three hundred men kept in a very low attic 'where they must stay day and night, where they perform their natural functions, and where they have no proper place to sleep, but must lie higgledy-piggledy with each other. I have seen other instances where a very large number of men were shut up in the cellars of such houses, some of whom had already been there five months, during which they had to breathe a very foul and sickly air'.[1] For this luxurious accommodation and for food of similar quality, the seamen contracted to pay 150 guilders from their pay, which was itself only about 120 guilders a year, so that the crimps well earned their nickname of *zielverkoopers*, 'soul-sellers'. That such conditions existed was not openly acknowledged by the wealthy burghers of Amsterdam, but their effect on the health of Klump's crew was to be a critical factor in the story of the *Amsterdam*. On the pages of the ship's payroll, names such as those of Jan Scholte and Metje Meijer stand out: these are the people to whom some of the crew are shown as indebted to the extent of 150 guilders. One such crimp was a certain Jan Jansz, to whom many of the *Amsterdam's* company were in debt and owed him a total of 4,375 guilders. One man, Huybert Aschbroek, even died almost as soon as he joined the ship, although presumably he had looked passably well when the VOC signed him on, but his decline had been rapid, and we find him struck off the

1. C. R. Boxer, *The Dutch Seaborne Empire*, p. 82

I. Contemporary paintings, both in the Scheepvaart Museum, of the VOC shipyard (above) in Amsterdam, where the *Amsterdam* was built in 1748, and (below) East India House, which still stands, and was once the Amsterdam headquarters of the vast Dutch trading empire.

payroll with the word 'dood'. Many, however, did not manage to get so far as stepping aboard. The frequency of their deaths in the city's waterside slums was sometimes even so high as to embarrass the authorities, and their problem was alleviated by quietly squeezing two bodies into one coffin.

The preparations for Klump's voyage were standard procedure, so that although there is no record for his ship in particular, the documentation in general is complete. As he stepped abroad his ferry, receiving the deferential treatment offered to a captain, the voyage would have seemed begun, and he would have been confident of sailing to the other side of the world and back before he saw that busy waterfront again. As his boat unfurled sail and pulled away into the Y estuary, past the crowded ferries for the crews, he would soon see on a nearby quay the warehouse of the West India Company, possibly stacked high with newly arrived cargo, packed in bales and chests, ready for hoisting to its upper floors.

On the starboard side were more warehouses, among them the East India Company's own, looking small among the nearby shipbuilding yards. Brick-built with wooden doors, it overlooked a quayside – now a fast urban motorway – and Klump would have been able to pick out the roof projections housing the hoists which raised the merchandise to its various floors.

In a matter of some ten minutes he would have been level with the great VOC yard, built on two adjacent man-made sandy islands, linked to each other and to the mainland by a causeway. On the shore was the VOC ships' storehouse, its tall outline dominating the city's waterfront skyline. The Company's love of stamping its insignia on all its property was here taken to extreme for even the weather vane was of wrought iron in the form of a letter A – meaning the Amsterdam chamber or branch – over the intertwined letters VOC. Separated from one end of this building by a wet dock lay the long VOC ropewalk.

It was in this shipyard that Klump's own vessel had just been built and launched. Already a pilot and skeleton crew had taken her to the rendezvous point off Texel, there to await crew, cargo, stores, and his own arrival. Although Klump had probably not yet seen her, details of her brief history would be in his papers. The directors had decided on her construction, together with two sister-ships, the *Hartenkamp* and the *Elswout*, on 2 April 1748. By October she had been launched, and Klump's colleagues – Skipper Jan Diderik Mosel and Captain Lieutenant Dirk Took – were also about to take up their commands with the same treasure fleet.

The *Amsterdam* belonged to the Company's largest class of East Indiaman – 150 feet from stem to stern and displacing 700 tons – and she came from a yard famous for efficiency. As early as the seventeenth century the company had standardised the size, shape and construction of their vessels, in order to calculate cargo and personnel requirements with greater expedition, though the 150 feet class had been a relatively recent introduction. Constructional parts were stored until a new ship was required, and even such a comparatively large ship as the *Amsterdam* could be off the stocks in three or four months, whereas a British warship of similar size required a year, or even two, to complete. It is even recorded that one was built in just over three months, in two parts, the separately constructed poop deck being slotted into position onto the main hull by floating cranes after the hull had been launched. Such a 'modern' technique illustrates the brilliancy of the planning which lay behind the Dutch 'golden age' in the seventeenth century, when the tiny Netherlands was transformed for a time into a great world power.

As Klump's ferry sailed into the Zuyder Zee, with the serrated silhouette of Amsterdam receding onto the skyline, a flat expanse of water and land, the one seeming to merge into the other, lay all around. In the distance were the roofs of scattered villages, and the sails of colourful windmills rose from the dykes. It is in such a landscape that the audacity of generations of Dutchmen can best be appreciated, representing as it does their constant battle with the sea.

The Zuyder Zee itself is no more than about seven metres deep and, studded with shoals and sandbanks, this inland sea is treacherous. The great East Indiamen drew practically seven metres themselves when fully laden, and taking them down to Texel was a task requiring skilled pilots and skeleton crews to guide them through the twisting underwater channels. A lead and line were in constant use, and an accurate chart was a necessity.

The swell would now have lifted Klump's small ferry, and with a swing of the tiller to starboard, it would surge northwards to where the *Amsterdam* lay. The trip to Texel could last a few days, depending on the wind, but Klump would have wasted no time wondering what his vessel looked like. All East Indiamen of 150 feet were standard in their build, the main variation occurring in their decoration and colouring. There were two main gun decks, with a complement of 54 cannon. Amidships, in the ship's waist, the upper deck was open to the sky, but forward it was overlain by the forecastle. Behind was the quarter deck, and in turn the after part of this was covered by a short poop deck. At the stern she would be splendid with new-painted wood carvings between colourful panels, possibly in red, blue and green, the lowest part ending in the carved fish's tail that was discovered still attached to the hull in 1984. In contrast the bow would not be ornate, except for the figurehead, which in the case of the *Amsterdam* was most likely to have been a great gilded or yellow-painted lion, representing the Province of Holland. Three tall masts, and a long straight bowsprit, would carry a great spread of canvas, and with all sails set she would look a splendid sight.

The ship herself would have needed anything from one week to six to complete the voyage from Amsterdam to Texel, because of the tortuousness of the navigable channel for a vessel of her size. Cargo, stores, armament, and sometimes even some ballast, would have to be stripped from her in order that she might make her way through the Zuyder Zee shallows; and to clear the sandbank which closed the Y estuary, recourse was had to *kamels*. These curious, box-like craft – so-called because they worked in pairs like a couple of camel humps – were submersible pontoons which lifted the East Indiamen the vital last metre which allowed them to ride over the sandbanks and travel to Texel where everything and everyone was put on board.

This bleak island of sand dunes, pounded by the winter gales of the North Sea, gave safe deep water moorings on its leeside for the largest vessels. There were warehouses of the Company on the island, too, but the bulk of the supplies and cargo came by barge from Amsterdam, from the barrels of beer to the great treasure itself, and were duly checked on board by the supplies officer and the chief accountant. Further provisions might be expected to be taken aboard at the Cape of Good Hope, but, generally speaking, everything that more than three hundred people would consume during the outward voyage would need to be loaded now. The quantity, even if the rations for the soldiers and crew were far from liberal, was daunting. In respect of quality, the food was strictly divided into that suitable for officers and passengers, and that which the rest of the ship's complement were expected to endure. Frisian butter of good quality and Edam cheese were reserved for the upper echelons and – oddly enough in view of its high modern reputation – cheap Irish butter was considered good enough for the lower ranks.

A huge quantity of paperwork was involved in these voyages, and Captain Lieutenant Willem Klump's excitement as he stepped aboard his new ship for the first time must have been tempered by the recollection of his share in this duty before he could finally set off for the journey to Batavia which was planned to last between six and nine months and take him half way round the world.

2

Embarkation

As Willem Klump walked the deck of the *Amsterdam* for the first time, both passengers and crew would have been wondering what sort of man was taking charge of their destiny. Wrecks were not infrequent in these long voyages on ill-charted seas where, although a seaman had accurate instruments to determine latitude, he was able to establish his longitude only by calculated guesswork. For up to nine months the rough complement of three hundred sailors and soldiers would need to be ruled with a firm hand, and it is not surprising that many of the Company's captains had a reputation as harsh disciplinarians.

Whether Klump was one of their number, it is now difficult to tell, but something of his character can be gleaned from the various circumstances we do know of his life. At home he seems to have been a thoughtful man, considerate of the opinions of others, for we find that he and his wife owed allegiance to different denominations of the Dutch church. He adhered to the tolerated Lutheran church, and she to the official Dutch Reformed, and they agreed before the voyage that in the event of their death, little Coenraad should be brought up a Lutheran like his father, and their daughter should follow the faith of her mother.

It seems likely that Klump himself came from a Dutch family engaged in the Baltic trade, for he had been born about 1715 in the small town of Mittau, now known as Jelgava. In this Latvian city, today part of the Soviet Union, he would have grown up in an atmosphere of ships and commerce, and the transition to a career with the East India Company when he was old enough would have been a natural one. At the age of thirty he had received his first command of an East Indiaman, the *Eijndhoeff* and had set sail in mid-December 1745 to make a voyage which ended a year-and-a-half later, in the summer of 1747, with his return in charge of a full cargo.

At the time of setting out he was already a married man, having taken as a wife twenty-four-year-old Margareta Schade. The ceremony had been in the Nieuwe Kerk (New Church) in Dam Square on 8 September 1743, and this building – restored in 1974 – still survives. In the same month of that year (on the 27th) he had been honoured as a freeman of the city in which he had settled, and when his new command also bore the name of *Amsterdam*, every omen might have seemed fortunate. Shortly after their marriage the couple had moved to the rented house on the Prinsengracht where their first baby, their daughter Elysabet, was born in 1744. The birth was in August, for the child was baptised on the twenty-first of that month, and their son, Coenraad, was similarly baptised on 8 July 1748.

Then as now, the Prinsengracht was a fairly prosperous part of the city. East India captains were not highly paid. Klump's monthly salary of 72 guilders was about the same as had been paid to the Company's captains a hundred years before, and to add to his difficulties it was the Company custom to retain a considerable percentage of this meagre pay until their commanders brought their ships home again – just to make sure that they did return. The same applied to the crew, who found it equally difficult to live on their pay, let alone make provision for retirement, or give a prospect of financial security to their families in the event of their dying on the voyage.

Human ingenuity naturally found an answer to the problem. A tradition of 'private trade' grew up among the Company's employees, in which more or less everyone took part, from the Governor-General of Batavia to the most junior ship's boy. And, unless this trading reached a flagrantly outrageous level, the authorities turned a blind eye.

Willem Klump's 'private trade' is not recorded, therefore, among the Company archives at The Hague, but in the municipal records of the city of Amsterdam itself. Here the legal documents of the eighteenth-century notaries record the plans, and the hopes of its people, as expressed in their debts. On 2 October Klump had visited the office of notary Arnoldus de Ridder to settle details enabling him to borrow 2,320 guilders from Paulus van den Bogaard of Delft. He seems to have been a welcome borrower, for next day he called again to increase the loan to 8,120 guilders, borrowing 2,320 from a certain Jan Groes, and 3,480 from Arnold Habich. There is no record of exactly what trade goods so much money was to be invested in, but since the loan was to be repaid with interest when his ship arrived at the Company's half-way station of Cape Town, he must clearly have intended to make his profit here. Even this large loan, however, did not fill the scope of

II. The *Amsterdam*'s Paybook for 1748–9 (above), still in the Dutch State Archives at The Hague, which lists all the complement of the ship: their names, home towns, sponsors and possessions, as well as the meagre wages due to them. Below is a cross-section of the Dutch East Indiaman *Noordt Nieuwlandt*, built in Rotterdam in 1750, which was probably very similar to the *Amsterdam*.

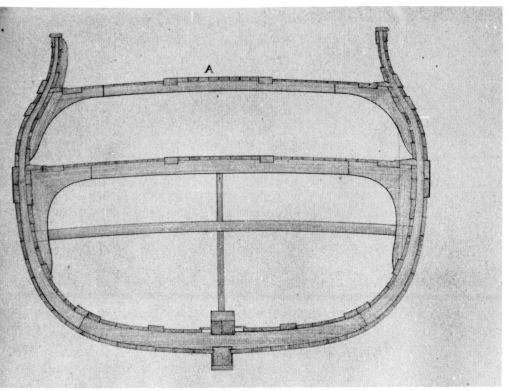

his ambition, for a day or two before finally leaving Amsterdam to join his ship at Texel he was again in the notary's office. This time he borrowed a further 3,900 guilders from Mrs Daniel Armenault and David D'Arnaud, engaging to repay this loan on his arrival at Batavia, where he evidently intended to sell a further consignment of goods. This meant that he had borrowed a total of 12,020 guilders – the equivalent of about £1,200 then. The Company Payroll for the voyage naturally records only the number of *kelders* – chests of wine for personal use – which were officially taken on board by each senior person. Klump had five, each probably containing a dozen bottles of wine or gin for consumption on the outward voyage. In August 1984 a lid bearing the carved initials WK, possibly coming from one of these chests, was found where it had fallen into the silts outside the stern of the ship. However, we may eventually know the cargo that he took for his unofficial trade, for that lies beneath the beach at Hastings.

Having sold the goods taken out from the Netherlands at a good profit, Klump and his crew would have used the proceeds to buy cheaply the oriental goods, fine silks, porcelain and spices which were in such great demand at home. It was a 'black market' which undermined the Company's monopoly, for although the directors officially tried to limit this private traffic to the few items which each man could bring back in his sea chest, the rule was impossible to enforce, for even the Company officials who inspected the baggage of returning seamen were a party to the fraud through bribery. The Company directors recorded with some bitterness that 'the senior merchants, junior merchants, skippers, officers, assistants, and all other persons in the service of the Company' were buying up and bringing home 'the best and finest porcelain, laquer-work, and other Indies rarities, contrary to their oath of engagement'.[1]

The *Amsterdam's* first mate, Lieutenant Martinus van den Hoet, also had a suspiciously small quantity of belongings officially recorded – only four wine chests and no personal baggage at all. This suggests that this young man, twenty-nine years old and a native of 's-Graveland, who was like his captain only a few years married – we have a record of his marriage to Lutske Douwe Douwese some three years before in Amsterdam – was also engaged in this illicit trade. The same seems to have been true of the other senior officers, the second mate, Jurriaan Bartels, and the third mates Jan Kwast and Jan Spek, who had only a single chest of personal belongings in addition to their wine chests. The rate of pay for mates had not been raised either for a century, so that they would have been in the same financial straits as Klump.

1. C. R. Boxer, op. cit., p. 201.

Pay rates in the service generally were varied according to a man's conduct, experience, and length of service, and on this basis Klump is seen to have been an average candidate for the post he held. Not so the several people whose jobs were to be a crucial weakness in the conduct of the ship in the weeks to come. Hendrik Brumleij, the ship's surgeon, and his two mates seem to have been paid rather less than their predecessors a century earlier, which suggests a lack of experience. Apart from performing amputations and other surgery required as a result of any battle with pirates or enemy ships, the surgeon was chiefly concerned with treating the various sicknesses directly arising from the conditions in which the crews of East Indiamen lived. In 1748 germs as the cause of spreading disease were unknown, and Brumleij would have relied on the theory of an imbalance or impurity of the four bodily 'humours' being responsible. This conception, which went back to Greek and Roman ideas of two thousand years before, required a correction of the balance by enemas, purging, bleeding and dieting, combined with drugs, stimulants and tonics selected from a limited and usually ineffective range. Amongst the objects recovered from the wreck in 1969 and 1984 were the broken pieces of drug jars in a variety of sizes, a glass pestle, and three syringes for giving enemas, and we can be reasonably sure that they formed part of Brumleij's stock. The surgeon was, by the way, expected to purchase some of his instruments and medicines from his own pay, which accounts for the curious fact that the payroll lists him as receiving three months pay in advance, instead of two in the same way as everyone else. The 108 guilders that he received were obviously ridiculously inadequate.

Another man who was to be greatly in demand on this voyage was the *Ziekentrooster*, Cornelis Pasmooij, who was also paid well below the rate common a century before. The job of this 'sick-comforter' was to serve as a substitute Protestant chaplain. Forty-three years old, he brought aboard only one chest of personal belongings and four wine chests, his low pay perhaps reflecting a lower-class background. The Company employed ex-soldiers, tailors, cobblers, weavers, cloth-workers and bakers among their complement of 'sick-comforters'. Pasmooij, with little or no theological training, would not have been allowed to preach sermons, or even to say spontaneous prayers. He would have been limited to a reading from a few prescribed texts. His duties comprised the repetition of a prayer at the short morning and evening 'service', together with singing a psalm and reading a brief sermon; visits to the sick and dying, with the reading of suitable prayers; and also practical help, such as drawing up a man's will.

It seems curious that the Dutch East India Company, so comparatively careless of their employees' bodies, should be careful of their souls, but the sick-comforter formed part of a wider spiritual strategy. By financing thousands of ministers, lay readers, and sick-comforters of the Dutch Reformed Church, the Company put itself in the front line of the fight against the militant Roman Catholicism prevalent in those parts of the Indies previously settled by the Portuguese. Trading links were more strongly forged in the wake of the church. Among the crew Pasmooij may well have attracted the kind of resentment that always attends a man of working-class background who yet enjoys the privileges of an officer's rank.

Generally speaking, the crews of such ships as the *Amsterdam* were a rough and loutish lot, well earning the description often applied to them as 'the dregs of Dutch society'. To sign on for such service was commonly a man's last resort. The engagement was for three years, and having survived the hardships and uncertainty of a six to nine months' voyage out to Batavia, there was every chance of their contracting malaria, dysentery, cholera or leprosy – for all of which there was no cure. Many were natives of Amsterdam, and it has been estimated that in the year before the building of Klump's ship, there were 41,561 households living in squalor behind the showpiece front of fine streets and handsome buildings recorded in the art of the period. The poor were very poor, tuberculosis caused by under-nourishment being rife, and even the stewed stockfish and maggoty biscuits of Company provisions were better than an empty belly.

It was, however, very much a last resort, and the Company directors had great difficulty in recruiting Dutchmen as soldiers and sailors on board their vessels. The *Amsterdam* crew included Germans, Norwegians, Swedes, Danes, an Italian, and even five men from Ceylon. Already under-nourished and sickly, they would have found transfer to the cramped quarters of the lower deck of the *Amsterdam* for months on end was no passport to recovered health, and, as we have seen, one corpse was taken ashore at Texel before the ship had even sailed, and another man became so ill that he left the ship and died ashore.

When conditions were so appalling, it seems strange that any parent should send his son to serve as a ship's boy, but economic necessity and the chance of rising in the Company service ensured no lack of candidates. There were three such boys, all under sixteen, aboard the *Amsterdam*, but one of them was not simply an ordinary crew member. Research in 1983 by Olaf Heyligers, chairman of the project committee of the Amsterdam Ship Foundation, has filled in many details of his background. Adrian Welgevaren was one of the four children of Boudewijn Welgevaren and his

2. The signatures of Willem Klump, Captain of the *Amsterdam*, and of his wife, Margareta (top); the Dutch flag and the insignia of the East India Company as flown by all East Indiamen of the Amsterdam Chamber (centre); and (below) the signatures of Andries van Bockom, the young Company merchant who was a passenger in the *Amsterdam*, and of his wife Pieternella who travelled with him.

wife, Adriana van der Houdt, and had been born in Delft, where he was baptised in the Nieuwe Kirk on 28 January 1734. The family was quite wealthy and of good social standing, and, when Adrian was three years old, his mother inherited from her father a house in the Nieuwstraat, in the small country town of Leerdam, near Utrecht. The decision was made to remove there, but soon afterwards Adriana died in childbirth on 6 August 1737, and the children were cared for by an aunt until she, too, died in 1740. Two years later Boudewijn Welgevaren married Juffrow Johanna Spranger, though the family continued to live in the then fashionable Nieuwstraat.

Adrian's father eventually became an alderman of the town council, and had himself started his career with the Company in the 1720s. He had undertaken several voyages to the Indies, returning from the last, in the *Wassenaar*, on 25 March 1730. These had presumably been profitable ventures, and it seems to have been only the prospect of some more attractive business, as yet unknown, and the necessity of taking over his parents' estate, that ended his career at sea. It was natural that when Adrian entered his teens, he should think of starting the boy on his career in the same way. The fact that the *Amsterdam*'s Paybook mentions Willem Klump as directly responsible only for Adrian amongst the ship's boys suggests that his father came to a private financial arrangement with the Captain to take him on as his cabin boy. The youngster, educated and well-mannered, would have had no need of the miserable five guilders a month that the Company paid its ship's boys. He would have had better food and quarters than the rest of the crew, and would have been somewhat shielded from contact with the rougher as well as the more sickly of its members.

The soldiers on board Company ships were of the same quality as the sailors, and we find them described by one writer as 'louts from the depths of Germany'. Their function, once transported to the Company fortresses at Cape Town and Batavia, was to guard the trading empire, and of course to assist in defending the ship itself if it came under attack at sea. The man in charge of the *Amsterdam*'s military complement was a thirty-seven-year-old bachelor, Sergeant Gerard van Hoeij, but he had other interests besides ensuring that his men were disembarked safely at their respective destinations. On 25 October 1748, just a few days before the ship's sailing, he visited the Amsterdam notary Jan Rijpland and signed a document authorising his brothers Abraham Caspar van Hoeij, a lawyer at The Hague, and Cornelis van Hoeij, to handle his affairs in his absence. While there, he also borrowed 6,400 guilders from his father, Johan van Hoeij, who was 'Premier in the Secretaries' Office of the Noble and Great Mighty Lords of

III. A contemporary painting of Batavia (above), now in the Rijksmuseum. This was the East Indies headquarters of the VOC in Java, now the city of Jakarta, and was the intended final destination of the *Amsterdam*. She carried 16,000 silver ducatons, like those in the lower photograph, which were recovered from the 1743 wreck of the identical East Indiaman *Hollandia* off the Isles of Scilly, as well as many silver ingots, to be exchanged for Asian goods for the European market. Dividers, such as those shown here, would have been among her navigation instruments.

the States of Holland and West Friesland'. This was clearly for private trade, and he agreed to repay the loan on his return from the Indies, presumably as escort to a group of homeward bound soldiers of the Company.

Perhaps the most interesting people aboard the *Amsterdam* from our point of view are the passengers, not least in that three of them were women, a fact which may have caused Captain Klump some qualms, since conditions so little suited to men might be expected to bear even more hardly on the sex which had had less training for the rigours of shipboard life. Andries van Bockom was travelling to the Indies as Junior Merchant for the Company to buy Asian goods for shipment home. In such cases a man was entitled to take his wife, provided that he paid her fare, and Pieternella van Bockom Schook was accompanying her husband at a cost of 300 guilders. It was natural that the young couple should not want to be separated, but what was less to be expected was that Pieternella's sister, Catharina, was sailing with them. Although a close relative, she was not entitled to a passage, but this difficulty was overcome by entering her on the ship's record as Pieternella's maid. Later in England both were described as 'very fine women', so that it is unlikely that Diderick van Buren, the sixty-four-year-old Company director who went down to Texel to supervise the fleet's sailing was deceived by the subterfuge. Like the 'private trade', it was something to which a blind eye was turned.

The cabins of such passengers as this Company merchant would have been on the upper deck beneath the quarter deck, and from here they could have watched the arrival of the large consignment of treasure on 31 October 1748. Company officials in Batavia, the Company headquarters in the Indies, which is now the Indonesian city of Jakarta, had that year requested a more urgent supply of silver than usual. The market was particularly favourable for the purchase of goods, and the Company, never slow to meet such a situation, decided to send silver bullion – the international currency – worth 4,800,000 guilders. Part of the sum was distributed among the ships of the autumn fleet gathering at Texel, the *Amsterdam*'s quota of 300,104 guilders (then about £33,600) being locked into twenty-eight metal-bound wooden chests. Twenty-four of the chests each contained fifty wedge-shaped silver ingots, and the other four contained a total of 16,000 silver ducatons. The contents of each particular chest of ingots was carefully recorded, together with their numeration from twelve to thirty-five, and it was also noted that each of the chests of ducatons, which were numbered from ninety-one to ninety-four, contained twenty bags, each bag containing two hundred ducatons. The heavy treasure chests were then carried across

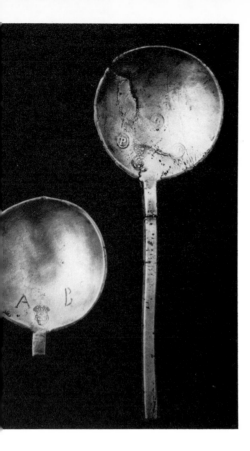

IV. Broken spoons (above), the one on the left bearing the initials AB, of its young merchant owner, Andries van Bockom, and, to the right, one with initials of his wife, PBS, Pieternella Bockom Schook. Below, a collection of recovered items, including a wine glass, glass cups, a tobacco box, ivory comb, clay pipe, buckles, ivory fan, and spoon.

the quarter deck to the captain's quarters where they were locked away.

Van Bockom's own luggage for the voyage would have been lodged in his cabin on the upper deck, together with his personal supply of wine. He was a young man of twenty-five, married to Pieternella only seven months before, and, since this was his first substantial appointment with the Company, he had little money behind him. Indeed, he had had to arrange a running debt of 338 guilders with a wine merchant before sailing, and had borrowed a further 262 guilders and 10 stuivers from the merchant Jacob Olzati to buy clothes and other necessaries for the voyage. He was a typical middle-class Dutchman; had studied at Leiden where he had graduated as a lawyer, and only subsequently had decided to become a merchant like his father. Pieternella's signature, neat and individually written, with well-formed letters, suggests a corresponding degree of education and also suggests that she was a reserved and tidy person. Her husband's signature, however, is large and flamboyant, indicating a more extrovert character, so that we can conjecture that the law was possibly never much to his taste and that he had eagerly embraced a chance of a career with the Company. Pewter spoons marked as belonging to both van Bockom and his wife have been found in the ship, and there were also some feminine items of dress which we can be reasonably sure belonged to Pieternella and her sister. The only other woman on board was the wife of an army lieutenant, whom observers in England noted at once as poorer in breeding and dress, so that these tasteful items are less likely to be hers. They include part of the quilted and embroidered 'petticoat', decorated with a heart and flowers design, of a once beautiful long silk dress, and parts of the narrow, high-heeled shoe, together with some decorated bronze and copper shoe buckles. Already a misty image of the sisters begins to form, which is more closely defined by an intricately carved ivory fan and a pair of exquisite artificial flowers of silk on bronze wire, as well as parts of some necklaces.

It is perhaps Catharina Schook, Pieternella's sister, who most arouses curiosity. Only twenty-two, and from a good family background, why should she have elected to leave the comfort of her parents' home for the hazards of the long voyage to Batavia? What was she to do at her fever-infested destination? Perhaps she was betrothed to a young Company official, and was planning to marry there. Or could it be that her sister Pieternella, having married a young man who seemed launched on a staid law career, was fearful of her new role as a merchant's wife? The company of Catharina, courageous and competent as the circumstances suggest her to have been, would have been a considerable reassurance.

36

The other passengers were of lower rank in the social scale. The man, Jacob Hal, was a Company army lieutenant of thirty-six, and his wife, Maria Monk, was three years younger. As the records show, she was illiterate, being able only to make her mark rather than signing her name. For some reason unknown to us, her husband seemed to have been in a great hurry to get to Batavia, but he was to be much disappointed.

It was even in the natural course of events early November before the *Amsterdam* was ready to sail, with all stores, cargo and personnel on board. Accommodation was cramped, even for the passengers, but for the crew and soldiers, crammed into the lower deck the situation was much worse. To worsen it still further, part of this deck had been partitioned off, apparently to take excess cargo which could not be stored in the hold, in typical Company disregard of the health and comfort of their employees. Significantly, part of that excess cargo included wine, and almost certainly gin, which were to play an important part in the loss of the ship.

At last Captain Klump received his final despatches from the Company, and called a final muster: he now had on board 333 people, of whom 203 were members of his crew, and the rest garrison soldiers, and five passengers. The ship's complement should have included a few more, but, as we have seen, he had already lost one man by death and another by sickness, and seven were absent, presumably having thought better of their bargain with the Company. There would be no waiting to make up the number, but the moment a strong easterly wind came, he would be off with the rest of the fleet on the first stage of his twelve thousand mile voyage. In this autumn season the prevailing wind is south-west, so that he must have thought himself fortunate when 15th November dawned bright with a fresh, cold easterly breeze. The order was given, the crew leapt into action. Sails were unfurled and the cables slipped, the *Amsterdam* was on her way.

3

The Voyage

The easterly wind probably seemed steady as the *Amsterdam* punched her way through the small waves off Texel into the heaving ocean swell of the North Sea, but it soon veered to the north-west and blew onshore. This was a situation of some danger, for Klump could neither continue on course against the wind nor sail back to Texel, and he was forced to drop anchor. The delay itself would not have yet seemed serious, and his main preoccupation would have been to keep his ship's company up to the mark, ready to take advantage of the first sign of an easterly wind and resume his passage through the English Channel en route for Cape Town.

Many of the soldiers aboard would never have been to sea before, but since they had to form part of the crew for the duration of the voyage, they would have plenty to learn about handling a ship in those days of waiting, and many would have been too seasick to cause trouble. Divided into three divisions of about a hundred, the crew took four-hourly watches, then went below to the lower deck, where their hammocks were hung and their sea chests stood. Here the only natural light filtered through the gratings in the deckhead above or came through the open gunports, and when the latter main source of light was cut off by the closing of the ports in bad weather, candles and lanterns would be needed as the men groped their way to rest among the monster 12 lb cannons of Swedish make, with which the ship had been fitted.

The Company had no great opinion of its crews. One report described them as behaving 'like wild boars. They rob and steal, get drunk and go whoring so shamelessly that it seems to be no disgrace with them'.[1] It followed that they must be treated 'like untamed beasts, otherwise they are

1. C. R. Boxer, op. cit., p. 70.

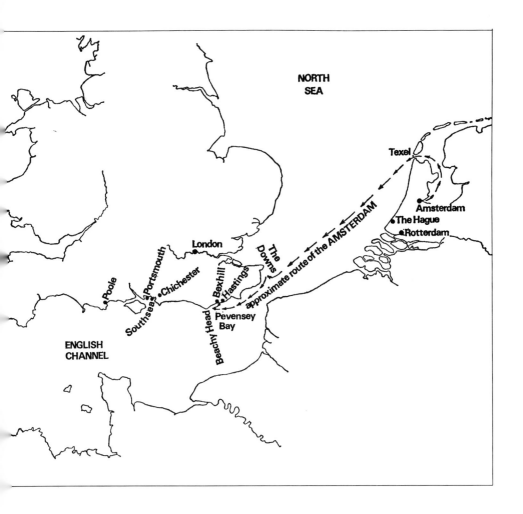

3. The probable route of the *Amsterdam*. She sailed from Amsterdam to her deep water mooring off the island of Texel in October 1748, and it was here that her crew joined her, and the cargo and stores were loaded. After two abortive starts, she finally began her maiden sea voyage on 8 January 1749, probably reaching the Downs the next day. Thereafter she encountered a very severel gale in the Channel, and about 23 January she edged into Pevensey Bay where her rudder was torn off after she struck the seabed. With about fifty of her people dead, the crew apparently mutinied, and she was beached near Hastings on 26 January 1749.

capable of wantonly beating up anybody'.[1] It was also noted that 'The least and lowliest person on board must be ready on the slightest nod or command of any superiors, to do everything he is told without grumbling. At any show of reluctance he is threatened and beaten with the rope's end.'[1] Whether in the heat of a tropical sun or in a winter's gale, the men must be ready to clamber in the shrouds or along the yardarm to tackle those billowing cream-coloured sails, and even in port there was little leisure since theirs was the task of loading and unloading the ship.

The scale of punishments was severe, the rope's end being the least of them. For theft a man could have his hand nailed to the main-mast; fighting and brawling earned fifty lashes with the 'cat'; and the penalty for homosexuality or murder was death, the culprit usually being thrown overboard tied to his accomplice or victim. Some officers were renowned for brutality for comparatively light offences, and at least one captain of an East Indiaman was tracked down by his crew after they had been paid off and beaten until his body was literally a 'jelly'. Mutiny was not frequent, however, since the rebels seldom included the men who were sufficiently trained to navigate a ship and bring it into port safely once it was in their hands. When one did occur, the consequences were usually disastrous for everyone involved.

The crews being for the most part illiterate, such accounts as we have are from the biased viewpoint of the Company itself, or from merchants or officers, and some chance recoveries from the *Amsterdam* suggest that the 'wild boars' were very much men after all. Amongst the finds are some bone dice, and a number of marbles, some actually made of marble and others of glazed pottery, for use in gaming, although playing marbles on board a rolling ship would not seem the easiest of exercises. One man seems to have had a flute for his own and his companions' amusement, and others spent their few idle hours sitting on their sea chests close against the open gunports carving objects of wood or bone, and decorating their possessions. Especially talented was probably Jan Aalders, the young seaman from Amsterdam who scratched a beautifully drawn ship in full sail in the bowl of one of his pewter spoons.

On 19th November, four days after her first sailing, the north-west wind veered and the *Amsterdam* slipped back into Texel, a pilot coming on board to guide her safely to port. It must have seemed a premature decision, for the next day – Wednesday, 20 November – the wind started to move back into the right quarter, and by the Thursday it was full east. Klump hastened to

1. C. R. Boxer, op. cit., p. 70.

seize this opportunity and set out again at once, only to find within hours that the wind was veering north-east again, and that his ship was caught in exactly the same predicament as before, pinned down close to the Dutch coast by the onshore wind. This time it was two weeks before Klump could ease his vessel back into Texel, and, with advancing winter, the days were growing ever shorter and colder. Tempers would have grown shorter, too, in the frustration of the delay, and matters were not eased by a storm which hit the coast about 14 December. The wind still remained onshore, and Christmas came and went with the *Amsterdam* still lying at her anchorage. So near and yet so far from their families and friends, those on board, and perhaps especially the women passengers and the ship's boys, away from home for the first time, must have endured it with mixed feelings. Klump and his officers may well have found some compensation in carousing with their colleagues on the other Company ships, for there were now six East Indiamen at Texel.

For the crew on board there could be no relaxation of routine, but work was always lightened by the sea shanties which followed the rhythm of their work in answer to the commands of their officers, which were themselves sung or chanted. A rare report from the lower deck of another ship of the period records that 'hoisting sails and each hard task had its own special song; and while the chant sounds, I admit, rather repulsively pleasant, it is really useful and lightens work'. Nor were the 'wild boars' without something of an ear, for a passenger on yet another vessel remarked that most of the watch joined in the choruses 'with most correct harmony'.[1]

Life for the passenger, or for an officer, could be relatively pleasant. All met for meals in the captain's great cabin on the quarter deck, and were served with some elegance. The table was covered with a cloth, the food was eaten from pewter plates with knives, forks and spoons, and the wine was drunk from slender wine glasses. Fragments of Chinese porcelain cups and saucers were also found in the ship in 1969 and 1984, and indicated that the officers and passengers took tea together. The cook and his mates worked on a well-organised schedule to produce three meals a day, breakfast at eight in the morning, a main meal at noon and supper at six in the evening. At the captain's table the fare would vary little from what would have appeared on a gentleman's table ashore, allowing for the fact that fresh food stores would soon have been exhausted in these days before refrigeration. The skull of a cow, recovered in 1969, shows that this animal was probably alive, so that they would have had fresh milk. A neat hole through the bone into the brain

1. C. R. Boxer, 'The Dutch East Indiamen . . .' in *Mariner's Mirror*, 1963, vol. 49, pp. 101–2.

cavity shows that someone had expertly put the animal out of its misery at some time during the shipwreck. In 1984 a few chicken bones were also found, and suggest a hencoop on the poop deck to supply eggs. The crew fed more simply. A typical morning meal would have been hot groats – a porridge of crushed barley, oats or wheat – cooked with prunes and helped down with a seasoning of butter. At midday there might be a serving of white pease, and a dish of stockfish – cod, or some other fish of the same family, cut open and dried in air without the addition of salt – with a little butter and perhaps some mustard to give it a degree of flavour. A barrel containing fish bones, found in 1984, shows how at least some fish was stored. Twice a week bacon, or salt pork, or beef, would take the place of fish, and the hind leg bones of pigs found in 1984 probably came from barrels in the stores. The evening meal tended to consist of whatever had been left over from the morning and midday sitting. Wine, beer and water are listed as on issue to the men, but the quantity is not noted, and we can assume for ourselves that the supply of wine would be likely to be limited to a warming daily 'tot'. The only other food listed by the Chief Accountant's Journal as held in quantity aboard was, as one might expect in a Dutch ship, cheese.

Immediately after Christmas there were further storms, and it was not until 6 or 7 January that the wind at last moved from the south-west and the Company fleet set sail on an eastern breeze. Two Indiamen, the *'t Pasgeld* and the *Overschie* sailed from off the Isle of Goeree on the 7th, and on Wednesday the 8th January, the *Amsterdam* herself set sail once more, this time in company with five others – *'t Huis te Manpad, Sparenrijk, Haarlem*, and her two newly built sister ships *Hartenkamp* and *Elswout*. This time the Dutch coast was safely cleared and by the next day, all were in the safety of the Downs – the sheltered anchorage which lies between the little town of Deal on England's Kentish coast and the treacherous Goodwin Sands. Here they overtook the *Overschie* and *'t Pasgeld*, which had arrived there the preceding day.

The logs of all the ships in the fleet have been lost, but the events of the next three weeks can be fairly accurately reconstructed from chance references in contemporary letters and newspaper reports. The arrival of the *Amsterdam* and the rest of the fleet in the Downs was recorded in the Dutch press, so that Klump's wife must have breathed a sigh of relief that the Fleet had safely sailed, just as did the relatives of all the others on board. There was also an English observer at Deal who reported the movement of all shipping in the Downs for newspapers, and he recorded the arrival of several unidentified vessels on Saturday, 9 January, and saw on the Monday that they had left during the night.

The wind was once more about to change, however, and it was next to impossible to urge these ponderous, square-rigged East Indiamen forward into such a wind as now came up from the south-west. Klump might well despair of ever getting his ship through the English Channel, as he spent the next few days beating back and forth, making ever less headway. At first the wind was comparatively weak, though chill and bringing rain with it, but when on Thursday 16 January the dawn came grey and wet, and the wind began to freshen and break the tops of the waves, Klump's experience would have told him that a gale was on the way. Ahead, the captain of the *Pasgeld* later reported rough weather near the Isle of Wight on that day, and he and the captain of the *Overschie* decided to run for the safety of Portsmouth, a harbour often used by the East India fleets. Unfortunately, Klump lay too far east, probably off Rye, to be able to join them. The seas were soon mountainous, and all furniture and sea chests, not to speak of the great cannon, had to be firmly secured to prevent their breaking loose. The gunports would have been firmly closed, so that apart from the hatches and a few small ventilation ports in the side of the ship, fresh air was now excluded as securely as daylight from the lower deck. There was no means of heating either, so that when the men came off watch cold, wet and exhausted, having spent four hours trimming the few unfurled sails in such a fashion as to enable the ship to make a little headway, nothing awaited them except cold semi-darkness. The galley would not even be able to offer hot drinks in such weather.

Not surprisingly, men who had already had their resistance weakened by their spell in the hands of the 'soul-sellers' of Amsterdam were not likely to remain long on their feet in such circumstances. A story has been handed down in Hastings that a specific disease, referred to as either 'black' or 'yellow' fever, was responsible for the high number of deaths. More and more men became ill, incapable even of going forward to the ship's heads – the primitive sanitary arrangements situated in the openwork of the bow. It is true that, had they reached them, they would have been washed away, but it must have meant that the atmosphere in the lower deck became nauseating. As the intensity of the gale continued, they began to die in growing numbers, and those who were not suffering from any specific sickness also began to succumb simply from cold and exhaustion, while yet others were washed overboard during their spells of duty. The death of Gerard van Hoeij who was in charge of the soldiers must have been a particularly depressing loss.

Ahead of the *Amsterdam*, the *Pasgeld* and *Overschie* hardly fared better. Though now close in to the Isle of Wight, they were undergoing a heavy hammering, a local report concisely recording that 'it blows hard, and thick weather'. Both ships were wallowing in the mountainous seas, their rise and fall being so great that both struck the sea bed, and the less fortunate *Overschie* had her rudder torn off. Early on Saturday she dragged her anchors and was driven ashore between Eastney Point and Southsea Castle. Watchers on the shore had seen her coming in from the direction of St Helens, apparently making for the calmer water of Spithead, but the tide was so high at the time, owing to the force of the gale, that she was beached. When the tide went down five feet of sand had built up round her hull, and it seemed impossible that she should ever be refloated.

The gale stands out as one of the worst ever recorded, and the horrors of their voyage proved too much for many of the Company soldiers aboard the *Overschie*. They slipped over the ship's side and ran away, hoping to make their way back to Holland later unobserved. Those that remained were perhaps more used to such storms, and remained at their posts. The officers, concerned for the safety of the treasure on board, had it taken off and placed with other ship's valuables in a tent on Southsea Common. Tents not being among a ship's normal equipment, it seems probable that the sailmaker used his ingenuity to contrive one out of spare sails. A detachment of the crew was then set to guard it with drawn cutlasses, which suggests that the Dutch officers had formed a very accurate idea of what was in the minds of the Portsmouth population. Their minds at rest as to the safety of the Company treasure, the officers then set to work to find a way of refloating their vessel while the gale continued to rage down the Channel.

News of disaster poured in from all over southern England during this storm. On 20 January unprecedentedly heavy rain, together with very violent thunder and lightning was reported from Bristol. A British naval sloop, the *Porcupine*, caught like the Dutchmen off the Isle of Wight was driven upon a lee shore by 'a violent storm of wind', and when three anchors failed to hold their position, the cables had to be cut. Next her topsails were cut away, in an attempt at least to slow the speed of the ship's drive to destruction ashore. Only the miraculous shift of the wind to the south saved them at the last moment. On the same day that the *Porcupine* gratefully found searoom again, the *Pasgeld* arrived in Portsmouth a few miles away.

There was no improvement on 21 or 22 January. Barnstaple in Devon suffered 'as violent a storm of wind as has been known in the memory of man', and the effect of the 'spring' tides which occur at this time of year was so far accentuated by the force of the gale behind them that in Appledore, in the same county, the sea defences were smashed and a whole street of houses beyond them washed away, many of the inhabitants being drowned. The damage was estimated at £3,000. Even as far eastward as Deptford, in London's dockland, the high winds caused trouble and served to fan the blaze in a new victualling house, a note of comedy being added by the fact that only beer was available as an extinguisher.

Gosport, near Portsmouth, suffered severely on 22 January, when thunder, lightning and hail added their terrors to the wind which continued all day and most of the night. Even here, in what was a relatively safe anchorage, four warships broke loose from their moorings, and one of them – the *Anson* – ran so headlong ashore that it took close on a hundred men to shore her up when the tide turned, so that she could be refloated next day. From Bristol, where one of the highest tides known flooded the lower part of the town, to Folkestone in Kent, where the tide tore the beach away, it was the same story, and all over Britain there were tales of at least fields inundated by swollen rivers or impassable roads. Kent had double the usual January rainfall and low-lying areas of Hastings were put under water.

During these days the *Amsterdam* was bravely battling the storm, and on about 23 January edged her way into Pevensey Bay, shown in Company charts as a safe anchorage within the shelter of the high, chalky promontory of Beachy Head. But the *Amsterdam* had not managed to get far enough into the bay to escape the force of the gale when she suddenly settled in a trough between waves, and there was a bump and a rending sound as her rudder was torn off. She had obviously struck the seabed, and Klump's dilemma was a terrible one as his ship began drifting north-east towards the shore, quite out of control. In a little while the houses of the then small village of Bexhill could be seen through the mist and spray, and Klump gave the order to drop anchor, hoping still to ride out the gale. He was surely justified in thinking that, after eight days, it would soon blow itself out and he would be able to make for Portsmouth and its repair yards.

His hopes were not realised. The gale went on, and for those aboard the *Amsterdam* it must have seemed hell without end. From the very beginning of the storm the crew had been dying off at an average rate of five men a day, and Klump's only consolation must have been the strength of his new-built vessel. Little else could have withstood the pounding of such seas day after day, for naturally at anchor the force of the waves would break over her with greater strength than ever. Ashore there was a lively interest in the crippled ship out in the bay. Five miles to the east lay the fishing port of Hastings, a cluster of half-timbered houses and cottages behind the curious high netting sheds on the sea front. Neither fishing nor their happy alternative occupation of smuggling were feasible in such weather, and the men had little else to do but watch the *Amsterdam*. Perhaps moved by fellow feeling for those aboard, and probably by the thought of possible salvage fees, some of the bravest spirits manned a boat and put out to her to offer assistance. Klump was appreciative but firm in his intention to try to reach Portsmouth as soon as the gale abated. The fact that the Hastings boat had been able to put out suggests that there may have been a slight lull to encourage his optimism.

If Klump slept at all that Saturday night, it must have been with a heavy heart that he woke on the Sunday – 26 January – to find the dawn dark and grey, and the wind blowing appreciably harder than on the previous day. More gigantic than ever, the waves smashed down on the captive ship, rolling about under bare poles. We do not know exactly what happened next, except that at some point the morale of the men finally broke. In the past ten days fifty of their number had died, and as the men still on their feet huddled together in muttered consultation below deck they were surrounded by almost as many again who lay sick and dying of exhaustion in the damp and cold. The ship was little more than a floating coffin. If Klump's orders were obeyed, it would indeed be a skeleton crew, if not a ghostly one, which took the ship into Portsmouth. They wanted the ship beached, and the courage to enforce their demand came from the excess cargo stowed by the Company so conveniently accessible in the partitioned-off section of their quarters. The partition was breached, and gin and wine flowed freely enough to dim the idea of the death penalty that followed a mutiny. They would not, after all, come ashore in the Netherlands where the Company's hand was strong, but in England where the Company was little loved and their chance of escape was good.

Although surviving Company records make no mention of a mutiny, contemporary opinion, as handed down in local legend at Hastings, is persistent in references to this having been the case. And the archaeological evidence supports the tradition, for two musket balls, distorted by impact, were found in the ship in 1969. Under lead isotope analysis in 1984 they were found to be of the same lead as the unfired VOC musket balls aboard, so that they could hardly have been fired by the English soldiers who later guarded the wreck, and there was no other situation except mutiny in which there was likely to have been shooting.

The crew would have known just as well as Klump that, if the ship were

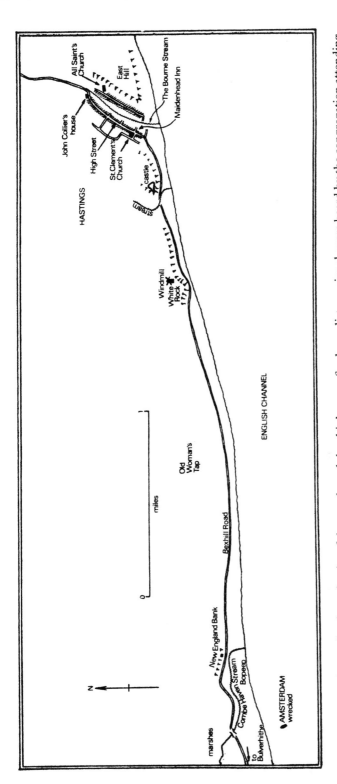

4. Hastings lies three miles from the site of the wreck, and the ship's guns, fired as a distress signal, were heard by the congregation attending Evensong in St Clement's Church. The ship's treasure was later stored in the town – shown here as it appears on an 18th century map – and some of the survivors of the wreck stayed in the Maidenhead Inn. St Clement's Church and John Collier's house still survive, but the Maidenhead Inn was destroyed in the air raids of World War II.

to be safely beached, advantage must be taken of the high tide to get her as far up the shore as possible, and allow them to use low water to get everyone ashore and unload the cargo. We cannot know exactly what happened, but it seems possible that the muskets were fired in a mutinous attempt to force Klump's hand, since no captain beaches his ship if he can possibly help it, and Klump could still have been hoping for a change in the weather.

One sinister find may be linked with this incident. In 1969 one of the mechanical excavators working on the wreck dug into the stern of the ship and scooped up the leg bones of a boy from the lower gun deck. We know that the other two ship's boys survived, so that these bones must have formed part of the skeleton of the cabin boy, Adrian Welgevaren. Four more bones, also from the lower half of the skeleton, were recovered from disturbed desposits in 1984, which suggested that the upper half may yet be found intact and perhaps indicate something of the circumstances in which he died.

The decision to beach the ship was made, but in the interval before the high tide due at three o'clock that afternoon Klump sat down, with an undoubtedly heavy heart, to instruct the supercargo – the officer in charge of the cargo – to write a statement describing the circumstances of its at least partial loss. Then, he called his officers one by one to his cabin to read and append their signatures. At the same time, or more probably later, since at this moment he still hoped to save his ship, he prepared (as we know from VOC records) a statement of the circumstances of the loss of the vessel itself for the Company directors. Neither document survives, but the dismal record of deaths on board and of the savagery of the gale may be easily imagined.

About an hour before the height of the tide either the anchor was raised or the cable was cut, and the *Amsterdam* rose once more to the sea. The ship's carpenter may well have rigged up a jury rudder to serve well enough to enable the ship to be guided towards the safest-looking stretch of beach. Closer and closer she drifted until the waves could be seen breaking on the shingle, and Klump ordered some of the cannon to be run out and fired as a distress signal. Miraculously the ship passed unscathed through a gap between two underwater rock outcrops which lay less than a stone's throw on either side of her, for either could have ripped her bottom out had she touched them. Instead, she ground gently to a halt within a matter of minutes on the intervening sandy clay strip, and lay at rest about two hundred metres from high watermark.

Klump must have congratulated himself, but if he had only known it, his troubles had merely half begun. The beaching of the ship had gone almost

V. A close-up of the musket balls found in the ship in 1969 (above), possibly flattened when fired during the mutiny preceding the loss of the ship at Hastings. Large quantities of such ammunition were carried aboard the *Amsterdam*, as can be seen from the pile (below) found on the sea bed in 1984, where they have spilled from their barrel container.

unnoticed, for having found the captain so firm in his intentions of reaching Portsmouth, and having seen for themselves that the ship was completely sound, the fishermen of Hastings had lost interest in the vessel. They could not have known the aggravating circumstances aboard which compelled Klump to make his final fatal decision, and since the *Amsterdam* had so far survived there seemed nothing to stop her continuing to battle it out in the bay. Consequently there was probably only one man actually present when she came ashore. We can imagine him wrapped in his winter cloak and standing with his horse on the windswept beach, the local landowner, Sir Charles Eversfield, watching it all from a distance, and registering his disgust when he heard the drunken shouting which re-echoed from the Dutch ship.

4

Shipwreck

Evensong was early that day. For, in the eighteenth century, when sputtering candles were the only ally against the darkness within the little church of St Clement's, and the walk home afterwards through the streets of the little town of Hastings meant reliance on the dim glimmer of a lantern, congregations took advantage of every hour of natural light. Not that there was much even of that on this afternoon of leaden skies and a howling gale. Gusts swept strongly up the little High Street, tucked away between the east hill and the west hill, and built by a people who knew too much of the evil fury of the sea ever to want to have their homes facing out towards it. Set just slightly apart from the main road, on a little eminence, the church still stands, its walls a mingling of grey and golden stone. It is easy to imagine the rattling of the leaded panes in the windows, the lash of the rain on the glass, and the creak of doors striving to hold fast and keep the tempest from the worshippers gathered inside two hundred years and more ago.

Among them was Thomas Smith, the Customs officer for Eastbourne, seated in a pew rather more handsome than even the respectable rank of Customs officer then warranted. He owed his position there to his wife, who although her spelling was atrocious, was sister to no less a man than John Collier. Collier was secretary to the Duke of Newcastle who, as Admiral of the Sussex coast, was partly responsible for handling all shipwrecks on those shores of southern England. In his own right, Collier was also a solicitor with a very prosperous practice in Hastings, and besides having served as Town Clerk had borne the chain of office no less than five times as Mayor. His prospects must have seemed even brighter still, for not only was he on friendly terms with Henry Pelham, the Prime Minister of the day, but his own patron – the Duke of Newcastle – was Pelham's elder brother and next in line in the succession to the premier's chair in the dynasty of Whig politicians who then held England in their pocket.

However, on 1 October 1748 Collier was 'very suddenly seized with a sort of appoplectick fit and the palsy which deprived me of the use of all my left side, and which in great measure continues, and very much renders me incapable of buisiness'. His physician, Dr Russel, advised rest and more particularly that he should spend the winter at Bath, where the excellent medical facilities and a course of the spa waters would undoubtedly restore him to health. Collier took the advice, and summoned his sister and her husband to look after his house, built – after the fashion of fine houses in those days – out of sight of the sea at the rear of Hastings. The departure of so great a man involved a considerable upheaval, and he was particularly concerned that he should be kept constantly informed of everything that happened in the town which was his overwhelming interest in life. He charged his many relatives and friends as well as his personal secretary, Richard Patrick, to keep up a steady stream of letters. Since he was not short of friends, and had two children by his first wife and eighteen by his second (though not all lived long), his correspondence promised to be considerable.

Dozens of letters have been preserved, first by Collier himself, then by his descendants, and now by the East Sussex Record Office at Lewes. And so it happens that it is thanks to a man who never actually saw any of the historic events connected with the *Amsterdam* that we know so much about her shipwreck. It is a stroke of luck the more to be appreciated in that the newspapers of the time, and even the records of the Hastings Town Council, the latter perhaps with better reason, have no mention of the affair at all.

Thomas Smith, as Collier's brother-in-law, was naturally among his correspondents, and as he prayed that day in the little church the sick man was undoubtedly in his thoughts. Suddenly, however, his devotions were broken in upon by the sound of guns. In time of peace in a seafaring town that meant only one thing. Every man and woman of that congregation would know at once that a ship was in distress, and their thoughts would fly to the Dutchman out in the Channel, of whose condition such tales had been brought back by the fishermen who had been out to her to offer help.

With instant professional instinct, Smith pulled out his watch to note the time – almost exactly three o'clock – then, his cloak pulled about him, stepped to the church door. Among those who left with him, there would have been William Thorpe, the current mayor of the town, and Collier's personal secretary, Richard Patrick, who had only recently been writing to him that 'our town is at present very dull'. Running down towards the sea

VI. John Collier (above), a painting by an un-known artist in the Hastings Library collection. It was to Collier that his friends and relatives wrote the letters describing the loss of the *Amsterdam* which are now in the East Sussex archives at Lewes. A view (below) over the old town of Hastings, in Sussex on the south coast of England, which lies three miles east of the shipwreck site (arrowed).

BEACHY HEAD

PEVENSEY BAY

SHIPWRECK SITE

through the narrow passageways between half-timbered houses, some of which still stand today, it would not be until they reached the shore down by the fishing harbour that the full force of the gale would hit them. Here a shingle beach runs out for some distance, and spray and spume would almost blind them as they stood craning their necks to see the ship in the darkness of the west, where the dull boom of the guns, heralded by red flashes, drew their eyes.

Today a coast road bordered by a wide promenade links the wreck site with the spot where these eager watchers stood, but then it would have been a muddy track along which they urged their horses and carriages, with the lesser folk of the town following as best they might on foot. In such a sea it must have been difficult to tell exactly what had happened to the *Amsterdam* from the point at which they first sighted her, but as they drew nearer, they could see she was aground and in serious trouble.

The point where she struck is bleak and windswept, and the *Amsterdam* lay with her bow facing the beach, and with her high decorated stern fully exposed to the onslaught of the great waves which crashed into her, throwing up sheets of white spray which broke right over her masts and were carried by the wind on towards the shore. The excessive height of the tide was due to the winds sweeping down the Channel and building up an enormous volume of water, far beyond the usual levels, so that the sea seemed to be reaching out of its bed to throw the *Amsterdam* shorewards and batter her into nothing.

Curiously enough, this very spot where the *Amsterdam* endured her martyrdom is the legendary landing-place of William the Conqueror, just east of the little hamlet of Bulverhythe, and his 'dining-table', a flat sandstone rock on which his first meal in England was supposedly laid has been reverently removed to ornament the pier approach in Hastings itself. It was also a favoured smuggler's haunt, and the name of the little place called Bo-Peep, which lies a few hundred yards to the east of the *Amsterdam*'s beaching, is believed to feature in the nursery rhyme:

> Little Bo-Peep has lost her sheep,
> And doesn't know where to find them;
> Leave them alone, and they will come home,
> Dragging their tails behind them.

Which, being properly interpreted, is supposed to refer in the guise of Bo-Peep to the Customs officers, the 'sheep' being the smugglers, and the 'tails' being the contraband.

As the men from Hastings came ever nearer the ship, peering in the closing darkness for signs of life, and dreading to hear the cries of the drowning they would be helpless to save, the most unexpected sound met their unbelieving ears. There were shouts, but not of fear, and singing, but not of hymns . . . the crew was drunk, probably bawling ditties as if in a snug alehouse instead of trapped in a wrecked ship. As a Customs officer, Thomas Smith could not have looked forward to taking up his duties when the tide went down and made the ship accessible between the hours of seven and ten that night. The mayor, William Thorpe, with his responsibility for public order, could have had even less relish for the situation, as he saw the crowd which was fast gathering on the beach.

His misgivings were very soundly based, for it had been little more than a year ago that the *Nympha Americana*, a prize taken near Cadiz by Commodore George Walker, commander of the Royal Family Privateers, had come to grief on this very same stretch of coast. On her way to London, she had been caught in a gale and had struck the reefs off Beachy Head, near Eastbourne, at eleven o'clock at night. Her bottom had been ripped off, while the upper part of her hull continued ashore, ending up on the chalky ledge at the base of the cliffs, with all the 150 men who formed her prize crew still safe. Soon, however, the upper part of the hull broke amidships and the fore part overturned, throwing thirty of the men into the sea, where they drowned.

Beachy Head was the loneliest of spots, but the ill news spread quickly and an assembly of human vultures soon came scouring over the great shoulders of the chalk downs, scrambled down the cliffs and, with little heed to the dead and dying, except to strip them of their possessions, set to work on the ship's cargo of fine cloth and quicksilver. Even a woman lying dead with her two children crying fearfully at her side did not distract the attention of the 'wreckers'. And in the morning, the crowd was even greater. The Comptroller of Customs, and several other responsible citizens from Eastbourne, tried hard to control the greedy plunderers, who had broken open the liquor stores on board and turned the affair into a drunken revel, but without success. The inhuman excesses of that day are graphically shown in the painting, now in the Barbican House museum at Lewes. Sixty people died, and many others were 'with difficulty restored to animation' by those local people who arrived on the scene with more humane intentions.

It must be remembered that this was more than a hundred years before Sir Robert Peel's police forces were introduced throughout England, and in such a situation the local watch was useless. All that could be done was to despatch a message to London, as was done in this case, so that an official could be sent down post-haste with a warrant from the Secretary of War, under which all the soldiers camped nearby on the coast could be brought in to guard the ship. More by good luck than design a detachment straightaway ran into a dozen smugglers hastening inland loaded with goods from the wreck. They abandoned their loot and fled, but only to return with reinforcements the next day to attempt to recover it, and in the ensuing fight two of them were killed before the rest made off into the surrounding countryside. A few of the soldiers now themselves succumbed to temptation and attempted to steal some of the goods, but were caught and received as many as fifty lashes as a reward for their ill-timed initiative.

William Thorpe subsequently remarked with some bitterness that the *Nympha* wreck had 'destroyed the morals and honesty of too many of our countrymen' and his own words must have echoed in his mind as he scanned the faces of the growing crowd in the gathering dusk, and reckoned the few hours that would bring the *Amsterdam* within their reach. By about seven, although the waves were still creaming over her, the sea had sufficiently receded for the soldiers and sailors aboard to start climbing down her sides and wading to the shore. Those who were sober enough were only too anxious to take the first opportunity to escape from what had become a hell-ship, and hastened to make for the dancing lanterns of the watchers ashore. Not far behind them were the passengers, Andries van Bockom, with his wife and sister-in-law, and Jacob Hal and his wife. The women were most probably lowered over the ship's side in a cradle and then carried ashore by some of the waiting men. They left in such a hurry that, fortunately for us, many of their possessions were left behind. Even in the darkness and confusion, van Bockom's ladies were recognised as such, and were undoubtedly rushed off with him by carriage to the warmth and safety of the Maidenhead Inn in Hastings High Street, just opposite the church of St Clement's. Hot food, dry beds, fresh clothing and sympathetic ears awaited them. Maria Monk Hal and her husband were apparently instantly recognised in the gloom as plebeian, and their reception may not have been so warm.

On board the vessel Willem Klump and his officers now tried to organise the rescue of the forty members of the crew who lay, either sick or dying, on the lower gun deck. There were consultations with William Thorpe, the mayor, and also with Coppard, the Hastings Customs officer, both on this problem and on the general question of security, for all discipline even among the more sober of the able-bodied crew had gone. With twenty-eight treasure chests in his cabin, Klump would have needed no prompting from the mayor as to the possible intentions of some of those among the crowd on shore, especially during the darkness of that long winter night.

One man looking out at the ship that night already had his plans well laid. Anthony Watson was the leader of a small gang of Hastings smugglers – no small-time petty thief, but what we should now call a professional criminal. He knew Holland well, probably even spoke the language, and must have specialised in the unauthorised import of kegs of rum and gin, and chests of tea. Tea was probably his most profitable line, for it was the most highly taxed of all commodities, and it was estimated that almost 50 per cent of all tea consumed in England, even on the most genteel tables, was brought in by the underground route.

This time Watson was raising his sights to a higher class of crime. Crossing and re-crossing to Holland, he would have watched time and time again the fat Dutch merchantmen sailing down Channel to the Indies, rich with silver bullion. Giant ships compared with his own little craft, impregnable in their complement of guns and fighting men, they were the stuff his dreams were made of. And now one lay before him, vulnerable at last. While Klump consulted with the mayor ashore, Watson and some of his men made their way up the ship's side, and broke into his unguarded cabin on the quarter deck. The gleam of their lanterns fell on the insignia of the VOC, which was probably inscribed on the lids of the treasure chests.

Hastily, they broke open the lid of chest number 16, the nearest to hand. Inside were fifty carefully packed wedge-shaped silver ingots, each weighing $4\frac{1}{2}$ to 5 lbs, and then valued at £24 each. Only the immense confusion aboard during that first low tide can have allowed them to make off with all fifty ingots. Presumably they lowered them in sacks to their confederates waiting in the waist-high, swirling water underneath the gun ports, and then departed as efficiently and quietly as they had come, completely undetected by anyone aboard.

The storm was still raging, the tide was shorter than usual, and too short to allow a start to be made on moving the treasure and the sick men ashore. Those of the invalids who were conscious must have listened with dread to the renewal of the force of the waves as the water rose again. Cold and wet, the best they could hope for was rescue in another twelve hours. Meanwhile, the shadow of death lay on the lower deck that night, and the darkness was only fitfully illuminated by the candle lanterns lit for them by their mates, before they rushed off ashore or to raid the liquor stores once more. The candle-holder and part of the door of one of these lanterns was found in the excavations of 1969 and 1984.

Their captain had gone to Hastings to hasten the rescue and salvage operations, though we may assume that one of the senior officers would have been ordered by Klump to remain on board. Whoever it was seems to have been inefficient, but if there had been no one at all in charge, Watson would presumably have extended his operations beyond a single chest. As soon as he reached Hastings, Klump had a more formal interview at which Coppard was present as the Customs representative; Richard Patrick, Collier's secretary, as the delegate of higher government authority; and William Thorpe in his capacity as mayor, which was in those days no ornamental office, but one of practical command over everything within the borough boundaries. Following the established procedure in cases of shipwreck, they expected the Dutch captain to write a 'protest', his official account on oath of the reasons for the wreck. To their surprise, at this point the Captain produced the 'protest' already prepared by the supercargo, and witnessed by his officers. Naturally, since it was written a little before the final hours of disaster, and the captain had still had hopes of saving his ship, it seems to have been primarily concerned with the crew's breaking into the lower deck cargo before the ship ran ashore. However, it evidently also gave the reasons for the actual loss of the ship in sufficient detail for it to be accepted that the writing of a fresh 'protest' was unnecessary. Klump having duly sworn that the contents of the document were correct, the mayor then witnessed it, adding his own signature.

Food and shelter for the 280 men of his crew would suggest themselves as Klump's next priority, and there would no doubt have been offers of hospitality from private individuals or, in view of the number concerned, perhaps a warm, dry barn offered by a local farmer would have been welcome. We don't know what arrangements were made, and it may be possible that Klump counted on the wreck remaining whole and the storm abating, so that all except the sick could remain aboard. We don't even know where Klump himself may have stayed, if he managed to sleep at all that night, though the Maidenhead Inn, where his wealthier passengers were accommodated, seems an obvious choice if none of the leading citizens offered him a bed. However, we do know that he would have paid the bills in silver pieces-of-eight, since the Company had given him 200 of these coins as his cash for the voyage.

Of primary importance in the eyes of the directors of the VOC, at any rate, would have been the bestowal of the treasure, and Klump must have put the subject pretty high in his list of topics to be discussed with the mayor. With the memory of the *Nympha Americana* fresh in Thorpe's mind, there seemed a good case for omitting the formality of obtaining authority from

London. Instead, he sent a direct message to the officers commanding the troops stationed on the Sussex coast, urging that men should be sent to the wreck site at once. A troop of infantry was forthcoming with commendable promptness, but since they were foot soldiers and not cavalry, the difference between being sent and actually arriving involved hours of marching, and they would not reach the wreck until another low tide had passed, a fact which Thorpe was to regret.

It is hard to realise now exactly what wrecks meant to the coastal communities of that day, when the quantity of personal possessions a man might accumulate in a lifetime was terribly limited, even above the lowest levels of society. Then, as now, the majority would not dream of taking life, but as far as property went, a wreck was a natural dispensation of providence for the better redistribution of wealth. Something of the feeling these people had can be gauged from a play, badly written by a local Sussex farmer, which he had published at his own expense in 1746. He seems to have had no experience of writing, and so far as is known the piece had no successor, but it attracts attention because, although written two years before the wreck of the *Amsterdam*, it deals with the imaginary wreck of a Dutch ship on the Sussex coast, and tells how it was plundered. Did William Hyland have a premonition, or was it just coincidence? A measure of the play's quality can be gained from the introductory lines uttered by the character of a Sussex 'wrecker':

> Hark: Boreas doth ruffle and roar:
>   And will bring us rich ships on the coast,
> Some Dutchman with bow's on the shore,
>   And then it is ours at free cost.
> We'll bowze* and carouse** of the best,
>   The owners (not we) are to pay,
> Let the merchants (rich rogues) be opprest,
>   'Tis nothing to us, we'll be jovial and gay!
> *drink **sing

With a true Sussex man's sense of fair play, Hyland allowed a member of the crew to answer and object that this sort of thing was just plain stealing, but with equal Sussex bluntness, the wrecker's rejoinder came fast:

'Sir, you are under a mistake, and call things by a wrong name; we abhor stealing, but walk in dark nights to assist you sailors at such unfortunate times as this; you have a present instance of the case, so what we get we claim as our right: for who acts in any case without Profit?'

The crew member would not, however, be put down. 'I suppose,' he says, "*tis* customary with you on the coast to make plunder at such unfortunate times as this.' To which the wrecker adds, 'We need not complain of the country people's robbing us, for I can see we can rob one another.'

The robbery was undoubtedly ruthless, as Hyland indicated in the tall story he puts into the mouth of one of his characters:

'I once found a hulky fellow alongst the sea, and the dog had nothing good about him but a pair of new boots, which I could not get off; and rather than spoil the boots by cutting, I lopt off both his legs and brought home altogether, and hung them up in the chimney until the legs dried and dropt out.'

With the coming of daylight and another low water, William Thorpe found his fears realised to an even greater extent than he had previously imagined. The local smuggling and beachcombing fraternity were on the scene in strength that Monday morning, armed with long poles with hooks at the end to assist operations. George Worge, Collier's son-in-law, happened to be in Hastings at this time, and had gone along to view the wreck that morning. He estimated, in his account of the scene to his invalid father-in-law in Bath, that there were more than a thousand people assembled on the beach, despite the cold, gale-force wind and the heavy rain. Nor had all the able-bodied crew taken advantage of the previous night's low tide to come ashore. Probably calculating that, whatever the advantages of dry land, they did not include unlimited supplies of hard liquour such as they had on board, their fuddled wits had led them to disregard any danger in their position and stay where they were. Their drunken singing and shouting reached Worge where he stood on the shore.

As soon as the grey morning light allowed Klump to see his ship, his relief would have been great to see that she was still as he had left her, or seemed to be so. Even at the lowest tides of spring and autumn in the calmest of seas, the spot on which the *Amsterdam* struck is not clear of the water for very long, and in this time of winter gale, the sea would not have fallen below the level of three or four feet (about one metre) round the ship's sides. This would have concealed a slight change, the sinister fact that she was some inches lower in the sand than she had been.

Even without knowledge of this, however, Klump's heart must have sank, as he scrambled aboard and stood amid the pouring rain once more on his own deck. Perhaps he had already mentally discounted the drunken men, but he had planned to get the senior, more responsible men to get the treasure ashore smartly. Instead, when he had managed to collect them to detail them for the job, he found himself confronted with a demand that they should be paid ten per cent of the silver's value for carrying out this task, which was technically 'salvage'. His position was difficult. He had no power to grant such a demand, nor would the Company ever admit such a claim, yet if he returned a blank refusal, he would have the choice of leaving the silver on board to be plundered or calling on local labour, which would be an even simpler way of losing the whole consignment. In such an event, he could be quite sure that his livelihood would be gone, for the Company would certainly never employ him again. He made the best of a bad job and, it seems, agreed to the blackmailing demand, but wisely put nothing in writing.

This matter settled, the men entered the captain's cabin astern to start work. It is a tribute to the professional expertise of Watson that his activities seem to have remained undiscovered until this point. His method of forcing open the door of the great cabin must have been discreet, and his men must have re-closed the lid of the rifled chest, for it was not until this moment that the astonished salvage team found anything amiss. They made their report to Klump, and almost immediately the word was everywhere that the robbery had actually taken place during the previous night. This suggests that the movements of Waston and his men were not altogether unobserved by watchers on the beach, though they might not have been willing to inform on him officially. The storm shingle on the beach would never have allowed a cart to come right down to the wreck site, so that, heavy as they were, the chests would have had to be manhandled from the time of their lowering over the ship's side until they reached the trackway beyond the tidemark.

Two men could only just lift the weight of a single chest between them, and the attention of the watching crowd naturally focused on the procession which now staggered up the shore. There were many speculations as to their value, some put it at £60,000, others guessing it to be more, and others again putting it at less. As is usualy on such occasions, the guesses tended to be on the optimistic side, and from a cross-check of the Dutch and English records, it appears that the silver aboard the *Amsterdam* had a value in the currency of the time of about £33,600. Less, of course, the £1,200 which represented the value of the one chest emptied by Watson and his gang.

Once ashore the treasure was taken under guard to the Customs House in Hastings, and Klump could concentrate on getting his forty sick crew members onto the deck and lowered safely to the beach below. The mayor, who in his private capacity was an apothecary and surgeon, would have had no difficulty in recognising their fatigued and debilitated state, resulting from a long spell in the hands of the 'soul-sellers' before the start of the voyage, combined with the effects of enduring for a fortnight one of the worst storms of living memory. However, as we have seen, local legend still has it that the main reason for the death of fifty men on the voyage and forty more being carried ashore sick was 'black' or 'yellow' fever.

For the next few weeks Thorpe did his best for his patients, though we do not know where they were put or what the treatment was, nor how many (if any) died while in his care. There are no burials of Dutchmen recorded either at St Clements, or at the other parish church of All Saints. Burials of any kind were few, since Hastings was then a healthy if not altogether law-abiding place, and the check is easily made. I am indebted to John Manwaring Baines, the historian and former curator of Hastings Museum, for a suggestion that the last resting place of these men could be in the churchyard of St Mary's, Bulverhythe. Even at the period of the wreck the little medieval building was in ruins, and its disused, overgrown graveyard could well have been considered ideal for the discreet disposal of the bodies of those who had died of such a disease.

Another curious feature of the events is that the body of Adrian Welgevaren was left aboard the ship, apparently on the lower gun deck. Maybe he was moved there because he contracted the fever, maybe he got trapped there in the course of the mutiny. It is possible that the upper part of his skeleton could be recovered in future excavation, and might even yield some clues to the cause of his death.

News of the wreck had by now spread beyond Hastings, and had even reached the little village of Hooe. This lies inland, six miles to the west beyond the modern resort of Bexhill and the wealthy sea-front villas of Cooden Beach. The men of Hooe were intent on more than sightseeing, and they swarmed over the side of the ship and made off with a load of cloth. The promised troops were still not in sight, but the mayor of Hastings stood his ground and issued a warrant for the arrest of the Hooe miscreants. Surprisingly enough, and perhaps because they had expected to escape identification in the crush and now knew that their eventual arrest would be certain, they agreed to return the cloth. One of them, however, perhaps feeling in honour bound not to go home empty-handed, stopped a waggon and called on his friends to help him in robbing it. He was again unlucky for William Thorpe, who seems to have been indefatigable in his civic duties, had him arrested as soon as the report reached him, and clapped him into gaol.

Later in the day, as the rising water of the tide once more relieved Thorpe of the need to keep an eye on the wreck for the time being, the soldiers at length came marching onto the scene to take over its guardianship. It is easy to imagine the heartfelt sigh of relief with which he greeted them, but a few short days were substantially to change his mind on that point. For the moment, however, all was well. Captain Klump, too, with his crew, passengers, treasure and ship safe, must have set off on the London coach the following morning, 28 January, with a measure of satisfaction. At the end of the long, jolting ride he would be meeting Gerard Bolwerk, the VOC representative in London, who would arrange the salvage of the ship and the transportation back home to Holland of the passengers, crew, and treasure.

5

Salvage

It was not until 6 February that the *Amsterdam Thursday Journal* carried a brief notice that 'Before the Downes was lost the East India Company ship *Amsterdam*, master William Klump, destined to Batavia for this Chamber, most of the people and cash having been saved.' When the Company actually first heard of their loss, the archives do not tell, but rumour must have run well ahead of the formal announcement, and Margareta Klump, and all the others with relatives aboard, would have waited anxiously to hear whether those they cared for were among the 'most of the people' saved from the wreck. There were also many with a financial interest in the list of survivors, and the moneylenders in particular, who had provided funds for the 'private trade' on which so many on board the *Amsterdam* had intended to venture, must have trembled for their silver.

Meanwhile, as Willem Klump trundled along the road to London, the jolting coach halted every now and again by the already uneven roads having been potholed by the torrential rains, his wife would have had no idea of his plight, much though the continuing storm would have made her fear for him. On this occasion Margareta was soon to see him again, but in the years to come she was to endure many long months of waiting during at least four further voyages before her husband finally came home to Holland for good.

Klump's departure to the capital, though necessary, seems to have been a little premature. He left in the morning, and in the afternoon of the same day – Tuesday, 28 January – a barrel 'as heavy as any of the chests' was salvaged with other items from the wreck, and it was heavy for the same reason. It was full of silver. After it is recorded as having been taken to Hastings Customs House, nothing more is heard of it among the goods returned to Holland later. Whose was it? Its owner had about 11,000 guilders inside this slightly unorthodox container, and it seems likely that he was not Klump. The captain had, it is true, borrowed 12,020 guilders before leaving his home port – the equivalent of his pay for about fourteen years! – but it is incredible, if the barrel were his, that he should not have delayed his London journey one day more in order to see it brought into safekeeping, especially after what had happened to the Company silver in chest sixteen. It would also mean that his declaration a few weeks later in Amsterdam that he had lost all his money, or the goods purchased with that money, on the beach at Hastings, was merely a profiteering trick. No, weighing the evidence both ways, it seems that the silver was probably not his, and the very fact that it was taken ashore the moment his back was turned is suggestive. Possibly it had been taken aboard originally without his knowledge, and the owner felt compelled to wait his chance to get it ashore the same way. If so, he must have spent his time between the grounding of the ship and his successful extrication of his secret hoard like a cat on hot bricks. Further research may solve the problem eventually.

On arriving in London, Klump would have had no heart or opportunity for sightseeing. His first call after obtaining lodgings, would be at the home of Gerard Bolwerk, the main VOC agent in England. A respected leader of the Dutch community in the north-east corner of the City, Bolwerk lived close to the Dutch Church in Austin Friars, where he was a church officer. Although sixty-four, he was still in business as a merchant. He and his wife had had one son, a merchant like his father, who had died at the age of twenty-four only a few months before Klump's visit, so that it would have been a sad household that the captain entered.

Bolwerk was paid a retainer of 500 guilders a year by the Company to handle such misadventures as shipwrecks, and his duties now included the arrangements for the salvage of the *Amsterdam*, the safe transport of the treasure to the special security of the King's warehouse in London, and the return of the surviving crew to Holland. His choice as salvor was a Mr Whitfield, who probably arrived in Hastings during the first three days of February.

When Whitfield took up his task, the continuing gale would soon have dampened any optimism he might have felt on the basis of Klump's first account of the situation of the wreck. At the end of January and beginning of February the rain had been so heavy even in the London area that the swollen Thames had overflowed its banks in many places, so that river craft had been in danger of being swept by the currents into the fields and navigation generally had been difficult. Caught between the rain flooding from the skies

65

and the sea still surging over her at every high tide, the *Amsterdam*, was in a much worse plight than when Klump had last seen her. Waterlogged, she had sunk some way into the beach, though still no one seems to have recognised how rapidly she was becoming embedded. Actual plundering of the ship had been halted, however, by the English troops despatched to the scene, although this seemed likely to have been a mixed blessing. A local man, who had evidently tried to get into the ship, had been shot during Klump's absence, and the fact of a corpse on the shore produced legal difficulties.

Mr Tilden, the local coroner, knew that an offical inquiry was likely to inflame local feeling, the shooting undoubtedly being regarded by local Sussex folk as an unwarranted interference with their natural rights and tantamount to murder. By a fortunate coincidence, the coroner thereupon found himself totally incapacitated by an attack of gout. He asked Richard Patrick, Collier's secretary, to deal with the problem. No better man could have been chosen. In consultation with Tilden and George Worge, he examined the various aspects of the affair, and came up with a solution worthy of Solomon. Since the man had been shot below high tide mark, he had obviously been 'killed at sea', and therefore, since the coroner's writ ran only ashore, 'the death of this person was not to be enquired into by the coroner and jury'.

What really happened in the episode on the beach remains something of a mystery, but it seems likely that the English soldiers did explore the ship. Perhaps there could have been something of a hand-to-hand scuffle with looters, for another find in 1969 was a bronze cuff-link bearing the bust and inscription of William, Duke of Cumberland, the third son of George II. It is a handsome thing, and so may well have belonged to an officer of the English soldiers defending the ship, the choice of decoration reflecting the Duke's popularity among the army men of the time. He also enjoyed popularity among the civilian population, an attractive cottage garden flower having been named 'Sweet William' in his honour, but north of the Scottish border sentiment was less in his favour. As the victor at Culloden, he had fought the last battle to be waged on British soil, on 16 April 1745. He might be forgiven his prejudice in supporting his father on the throne against the claims of Bonnie Prince Charlie, but his subsequent burning down of Scots villages, shooting of prisoners and outlawry of the wearing of the kilt, earned him the sobriquet 'Butcher Cumberland'. It is remarkable that, although it is so small, the pair of this cuff-link was found in the stern area in 1984. The finding of them both does raise questions about the possible circumstances of their loss, and it is just conceivable that they were owned by one of the officers of the *Amsterdam*, rather than an English soldier.

The troops being on guard over the ship, Whitfield probably anticipated having more time to unload the rest of the cargo than he was to be allowed by the treacherous beach. At any rate, his first priority had to be recovery of at least some of the silver ingots from chest sixteen. He was not inhibited in this by legislation of the modern kind which means that deals with insurance companies by thieves are carried on, if at all, in the utmost secrecy. He called in the Hastings town crier with his hand-bell to attract the attention of all and proclaim at the top of his voice that, if anyone who had any of the wedges in his possession returned them, two pounds would be paid for each – and no questions asked. Oddly as it seems today, the procedure worked, and thirty-four of the silver ingots came back in the next few weeks. The difference between the reward and the actual value was large, but two pounds was two pounds, whereas the prospects for a Hastings man disposing of the wedges without discovery must have seemed considerably dimmer than when the daring robbery was first planned.

However, sixteen were still missing, and we may guess that this was Anthony Watson's share as leader of the raiding party. It was not long before Whitfield became cognisant of Watson's activities, both as regards the ship and his standard smuggling trade between Flushing in the Netherlands and the south-east coast of England. Some of his accomplices probably handed over information as well as their silver wedges, and Whitfield wasted no time in passing it on to the VOC directors of the Amsterdam Chamber. They were no less prompt in forwarding the details to the Zeeland Chamber directors, in whose territory Flushing lay, asking them to find Watson and the missing ingots. Watson was no novice, however, and evaded capture, neither he nor the silver ever being heard of again.

Smuggling is one of the curious border-line crimes. Even today it has an air about it which makes otherwise honest people bring in something from abroad which they could well afford to pay duty upon, simply for the excitement and 'prestige' of being able to boast of having done it. Two centuries and more ago, it had at once more virtue – in that the goods so heavily dutiable were unobtainable to poor, and not so poor, people if they were to be come by honestly. And at the same time there was more danger. It was all very well for a fisherman, financed perhaps by some of the local gentry and tradesfolk, to take his boat across Channel, crewed by his family or friends. What he brought back enriched everyone all round, and did the Government little harm. If he was caught, he and his men would find someone mysteriously appear to buy their freedom, might even find one of their backers sitting as a magistrate on the bench before which they were brought. Indeed in 1770 no less a figure than Edward Milward, a magistrate and many times Mayor of Hastings, paid £25 out of his own pocket to free a group of Hastings men awaiting hanging in London for piracy. The Customs officers were the common enemy of all, up to a point, and hunted men and contraband would find willing helpers to conceal the goods and offer a temporary refuge in homes throughout the countryside, not merely in the Hastings area, but all along the southern coast.

With these activities in mind, Thorpe was on tenterhooks until the silver treasure was removed from his mayoral domain about the end of February, and especially glad to be rid of the 'plague' of foot soldiers who were 'the greatest thieves I ever knew'. He certainly spoke with experience. Even while he complained so bitterly of poor folk stealing from the ship, he was himself acquiring bottles of French wine and, what is more, offering to resell them to Collier at a shilling (5p) each! It was, as always, a case of one law for the rich and another for the poor. Thorpe had not even to worry lest his overlord discover what he was up to. His Grace the Duke of Newcastle was himself laying claim to the best anchor and cable aboard the *Amsterdam*, regardless of what the VOC, as legal owner, might wish done with them.

What Whitfield, as the Company's salvage agent, thought of the Duke's claim is not recorded. The case of the *Amsterdam* must have been unique in his experience, as she bodily disappeared from sight day by day into the shifting sands of Bulverhythe and their underlying yielding clay. Local people usually know of such peculiarities in their beaches as sinking sands, and so on, but the beach here is quite reasonably firm to the tread, and it was not until this gigantic ship settled its waterlogged weight into the surface that this particular fault showed itself. Indeed George Worge wrote in a letter to John Collier: 'She stands in a good place, and in appearance quite whole, and may do so for months. But no possibility of getting her off. I Believe they will save every thing that is worth saveing.' The write-off of the ship at such an early stage as impossible to get off arose not from the character of the beach, but rather from the abnormality of the tide on 26 January 1749 which had driven her ashore. The combination of onshore gale and an extremely high spring tide had carried her so high up, that no tide in the succeeding days sufficed to lift her. It had been a once-in-a-lifetime situation. However, this would have seemed an even more powerful reason why the cargo should be the more completely saved. Yet by the ninth day after the beaching, Richard Patrick had written: 'The Dutch ship . . . still sits whole, and the plunderers speed but very indifferently, neither do the owners save any quantity of goods, for the ship is so much swerved in the sand, that it is impossible to get at the cargoe, the ship being always full of water.'

Part of the archaeological survey of 1969–72 was aimed at explaining the mechanism of the *Amsterdam*'s gradual envelopment, and it was only then that the thick layer of clay just below the sand was discovered. This yielded under the pressure of the ship herself, her 150 tons of ballast, and the water that filled her upper decks. As she sank lower, sand washed in with the water and ultimately came to fill her interior completely, and it is this sand alone that becomes a true 'quicksand' when disturbed by digging. In the direction of the most violent waves striking the ship, to the west, a hollow was actually eroded by the storm in the lower level of the clay, which was quickly filled up with sand and debris from the ship.

Nowadays the clay bed does reach the surface of the beach on the east side of the ship, where it can be seen at very low tides with a mass of hard blackened tree roots embedded in it. These roots are five thousand years old, and were part of a prehistoric forest that was growing after the last Ice Age when the sea level was much lower.

When Richard Patrick wrote of the *Amsterdam* as 'swerved' – a Sussex dialect word meaning 'sunken' – in the beach, the ship was about four-and-a-half feet into the surface. This was not so bad, but Whitfield's task was complicated by the passing of the period of low tides, which would not recur for a month, and by the continuing gale, now somewhat lessened, but still pounding at the wreck with waves which broke in sheets of spray and rendered the slippery slope of her deck a hazard in itself. On 7 February the weather turned colder and a thick fall of snow added further to his difficulties, although a day of heavy rain on the 10th washed this away. The comparative thaw was brief. Next day the sky was clear but the air was extremely cold, and as the tide went down the salvage men knew finally that they were fighting a losing battle. It was sixteen days since the ship had been beached, and she had sunk about eight feet, so that her upper deck was almost awash at high tide. They found that it was impossible to open the main hatches, perhaps swollen with water, to get at the cargo, which was still of considerable value and worth saving, even after having been awash for the best part of a fortnight.

The *Amsterdam* being a new ship and built stoutly to last, it would take too long to break through her timbers with axes, and great bonfires similarly failed to penetrate the saturated wood. As a last resort barrels of gunpowder were used, but the water had risen so far that it was impossible to place them accurately for the best effect. Gradually the forecastle, quarter and poop decks were destroyed, and even part of the upper gun deck nearest the shore, but the lower deck – now completely under water except at the lowest point of the tide – remained almost inaccessible. The battle with the sea was nearly lost.

That the failure was so complete does seem surprising, and George Worge's viewpoint is understandable when he wrote, just twenty-seven days after the wreck, 'either from want of skill or honesty of the agent or managers, there is very little done towards getting out and saveing the cargoe. They blew up one of the decks this morning.' The ship was now 13–14 feet into the beach, and another ten days saw her about 18 feet (6 metres) down. Thorpe commented in one of his letters to Collier that 'the ship is so swerved in the sand, that at high water the sea covers her, and at low her lower deck is under water'. On the morning of the day on which he wrote, 5 March, a large piece of the lower deck (probably inside the bow) had been blown up, but the fuse to the barrel of powder having been too dry, the explosion came prematurely and blew up the engineer in charge. The engineer was Christopher Nutt, and he was buried at St Clement's church a few days later.

This incident was the ultimate discouragement and salvage work on the ship gradually petered out, the cargo and stores being abandoned. As no copy of the ship's manifest survives, the exact content of the cargo is not known, but the Collier letters provide some information. The ship is said to have carried 'all sorts of goods' and to have been 'loaded with money, bale goods [cloth], and stores of all kinds'. There seems to have been a large consignment of 'gold and silver lace, and wearing apparel', and it would have been some of this 'velvet cloth, etc.' which the Hooe people had tried to make off with. There were also on board 'a great many thousand dozen bottles of wine' in chests. Part of her stores, which were recovered in 1749, included such provisions as butter, bacon, and beef, but the bulk was left untouched.

In 1969 some of the excess cargo was recovered from the lower deck, and this confirms the mixed nature indicated by the Collier letters. Bottles of wine were found, containing what had probably been French vintages, and heavy stoneware bottles suggestive of gin were near them. Just outside the ship, probably jettisoned as already broken during the initial salvage operations, was part of a consignment of clay pipes. We can be sure they formed part of the cargo, since all were unsmoked and had with them, in some cases still filling the bowls, a large quantity of the loose husks of buckwheat which had been used when packing them into their boxes ready for transport. Another of the 1969 finds, originally thought to be part of the cargo, consisted of five bronze 1 lb guns, manufactured in Amsterdam only the year before the ship set sail, and still apparently wrapped in their original sacking. Now there is reason to believe that they formed part of the ship's armament. In 1984, besides other examples of items of the cargo already found, we also uncovered in the stern area lengths of velvet ribbon, and thousands of brass pins, some still arranged as if in their original packages.

All that the Dutch East India Company actually managed to recover from the *Amsterdam*, therefore, was the ship's treasure, three chests of merchandise, and one ornate chest decorated with gold and silver facings. Gerard Bolwerk must have added up the total in some gloom, but from the *Overschie*, the ship of the same class which had been beached near Southsea Castle on the morning of 18 January, he drew more comfort. Also a new vessel, she had been more fortunate than her sister ship in being sheltered from the very worst of the gale which drove her ashore by the Isle of Wight. Her crew worked together with her salvors for a month to clear the accumulated sand about her, and on the night of 15 February success was theirs. It was the occasion of an especially high tide, one of the monthly mini spring tides, and the men knew this was a last chance. Much longer aground and even the *Overschie*'s stout timbers would begin to work open, and once she leaked seriously, she would begin to break up.

Except for those who had run away, the whole ship's company must have been involved in the operation. The great anchors were carried out to sea in smaller boats, each secured to the ship by a long cable, and then as the tide rose to its maximum we can imagine the crew beginning with tremendous effort to turn the capstan inside the ship to wind in the cables, and so pull her through the sand and shingle out to sea. Straining with all their might amidst rising excitement, they felt the ship begin to move, slowly at first and then sliding quickly into deeper water. Once she was free, a quick examination proved that damage had been slight, and as she lay at anchor all the cargo and stores removed beforehand to lighten her was once more loaded.

On the following Monday she made her entry into Portsmouth harbour under sail. It was a memorable occasion, for calm though the waters were, she made straight for the bow of a merchant ship in her path and carried away its head, and then she went on to strike another ship twice, first breaking its bow-sprit, and then swinging round to clash into its quarter. After that she settled down to make a quiet entry into dock for repair, but before she was eventually allowed to sail for the Indies, Gerard Bolwerk had to pay compensation for the damage. Even as an officer of his church, he probably allowed himself an oath or two on that occasion, and the language of the

English skippers at being so knocked about by a Dutchman needs no imagining.

Generally speaking the *Overschie*'s crew had emerged with credit, which was more than could be said for those of the *Amsterdam*, whose ill-reputation as mutineers had since been augmented by their behaviour ashore. The Company naturally wanted them back in port ready to despatch on another ship as soon as possible, and seventy-five of them were put aboard an English sloop at about this time. The captain, William Betts, for some reason, put them ashore at Dunkirk rather than in Holland, and the Company directors (who would now have to pay to have them transported overland) were annoyed and entered into lengthy argument over the payment due to Betts.

The rest of the ship's company remained in Hastings, and combined to submit an official claim in the form of a letter to the Company. They wanted the ten per cent of the value of the treasure which they had compelled the captain to promise them before they would assist in bringing the silver ashore. The signature of the captain, and also that of the first and second mates, was not unnaturally missing from this document. The Directors of the Amsterdam Chamber responded to this tricky problem by referring the matter to the senior board of Heeren Zeventien or Seventeen Gentlemen, and by writing at the same time to Klump in London, via Gerard Bolwerk, for confirmation that he had indeed made such a promise.

The Heeren Zeventien met at 11 o'clock on Wednesday 5 March, and quickly reached the unanimous decision that they would not pay the men the ten per cent, and quoted Article 45 of the Company regulations in support. This confirmed the provisional verdict already reached by the Amsterdam directors, and when Willem Klump roundly replied that he had 'not promised anything to the crew of that vessel for salvaging the cash' the matter was considered at an end. Six days later, on Tuesday 11 March, at an extraordinary meeting of the Amsterdam Chamber, it was formally decided to terminate all attempt at salvage. Bolwerk was to be instructed 'to dismiss as soon as possible the people who have been employed to salvage the goods from the above mentioned perished ship *Amsterdam*, as it is unlikely that anything more can be saved'. The directors had decided to cut their losses.

Meanwhile, in London, Bolwerk had been advised that the Company would do better to sell their salvaged ducatons and silver bars in the City than to ship them back to Amsterdam. However, the Company knew their market, and that the silver would fetch far more in the Indies than in London, so Bolwerk was instructed to return it to Amsterdam in several ships – for safety! Ten chests went in the *Elisabeth*; three more, as well as the

Captain Willem Klump's home (above) on the Prinsengracht, Amsterdam, and (below) a model made in 1747 of the *Mercurius*, a Dutch East Indiaman of similar type and date to the *Amsterdam*.

A lead barrel containing animal fat, perhaps butter (above left); two of the bronze guns (above right) and (below) an underwater photograph by James Lawrence of a stoneware jug *in situ* on the lower gun deck in the *Amsterdam* in 1984.

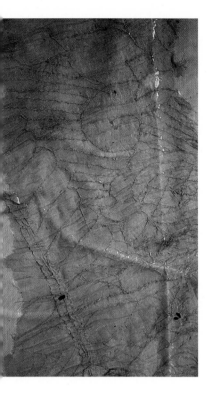

The ivory fan which probably belonged to Pieternella or her sister (below); the silk artificial flower (above right); and (above left), part of the silk embroidered and quilted 'petticoat', both the latter discovered in 1984.

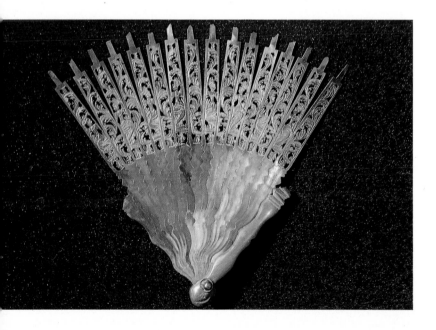

A low-tide view of the site from the diving platform, looking towards the shore, and the leg bones of the cabin boy, Adrian Welgevaren, together with two fired musket balls.

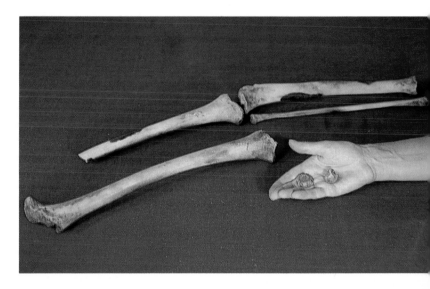

three chests of merchandise, in the *d' Unie*; and the rest were split among the *Juffrouwe* (i.e. Miss) *Anna, Maria Agneta,* and *d' Eendragt.*

Yet although the Company had abandoned hope of any really successful salvage, they could not quite bring themselves to let the ship go entirely for nothing. On Friday 4 April they sent instructions to Bolwerk that he should sell the cannons, anchors and cables; and also the ship itself. No record remains of any sale having been effected, although the incompleteness of the records does not make this surprising, but the point does have a certain importance. The lack of evidence of any sale is the basis of the claim to ownership of the wreck by the Netherlands Government, and if such evidence were later to be discovered, there could be legal complications.

The last link with the *Amsterdam* was severed by the Company on 11 March, when Willem Klump, and the first and second mates, Martinus van den Hoet and Jurriaan Bartels, were given permission to return home. Klump, in particular, would have been apprehensive of his reception there by the directors, since there would now be an exhaustive inquiry on which his whole future with the Company would depend. All three men were summoned to appear before the Company Examiner, Ian de Marre, on 8 April 1749 and the interview most probably took place in East India House in Amsterdam. At the same time they also applied to rejoin the Company if the investigation went in their favour. Eventually the Examiner announced that his inquiries were complete, and that he was satisfied by his study of the ship's log that the course of the ship and the standard of seamanship had been in conformity with official Company instructions, and the best that could have been adopted in the exceptionally bad weather conditions. The almost exactly similar beaching of the *Overschie*, in slightly less rigorous circumstances, must have contributed to his decision that the wreck had been beyond Klump's power to prevent.

The Examiner's report was accepted by the Company directors and, with the readmission of the three officers to the ranks of Company officers, ready for another ship and another voyage, it might be considered that the *Amsterdam*'s briefly eventful history was at an end. Not so, it had only just begun.

6

After the Shipwreck

In the preceding chapters I have often mentioned material from English records, which are the obvious source for information on the actual period of the wreck, but it is to the Dutch records we have to look for further light on what happened to those associated with the ship in earlier and later days. When the British Broadcasting Corporation's *Chronicle* film was being made in 1969–70, it was done in conjunction with the Dutch television service KRO. One of the producers, Joop Reinboud, included among his many private interests an expert knowledge of his country's history, and it was he who carried out the main research for the project. Three weeks of combing through yellowed manuscripts and vellum-bound volumes resulted in a report that exceeded our wildest hopes. Subsequently others continued the research, such as Dr Simon Hart, former archivist of Amsterdam's city archives, who took up the search for and discovered much more information about Klump. The initiative for this came from Vernon Leonard and Ken Wilkie of *Holland Herald* magazine, and it was they who went in search of modern descendants of Klump – a search crowned with success.

Where the facts which were unearthed applied to the earlier part of the story, I have included them in the narrative, but I was particularly anxious to know what became of the leading characters in the story, not least Captain Willem Klump and his family, and Andries van Bockom and his wife Pieternella.

We have already seen that Klump escaped any charge of negligence on account of the loss of the *Amsterdam*, and that he was free to return to his family with his mind at peace in the knowledge that he would be appointed to a new command as soon as one was available. All the same, lucky as he had been to escape with his life and his career unharmed, he must have been physically shaken by the ordeal, and it cannot have been pleasant to return once more to the offices of the moneylenders to discuss his borrowings for trade, made with such high hopes such a little time before. However, the Amsterdam money market was constructed to bear the brunt of many such losses, and we find that he was released from at least one of his debts 'since the ship *Amsterdam* on which he had set off as Captain Lieutenant, has come to be wrecked'. This is unlikely to have been philanthropy, and it is likely that the moneylenders were somehow insured against such losses, and that, with the exoneration of the VOC in his pocket he would not find too much difficulty in negotiating fresh loans when his new ship was ready.

His next ship was the East Indiaman *Ruysckenstein*, scheduled to sail with the Christmas fleet of 1750, and this time he sailed from Texel on 4 December and completed the eight-month voyage without mishap. He made the usual stay at the Cape of Good Hope to take on certain supplies and arrived at Batavia on 12 August 1751, no doubt delighted that he had this time lost only seven men in 12,000 miles of sailing, instead of seven times that number on his previous Channel trip. His stay in Batavia was brief, a matter of weeks, and his return voyage, for reasons we do not know, was made as commander of another ship, the *Haarlem*.

By 8 July 1752, nineteen months since he had set out, he was back in Amsterdam with Margareta, and their children Elysabet and Coenraad. During this leave a second daughter, Anna Wilhelmina was born, and was baptised at their home by a pastor of the Lutheran Church in Amsterdam on 10 October 1753. Seven weeks later, having this time had seventeen months at home, he set out again in the *Bevalligheid* (the 'Grace'). This fresh voyage was obviously not such plain sailing as its predecessor, since he took twelve months to get to Batavia on 13 December 1754, but though the weather may have been rough, he had no trouble with sickness and only one man died. He made an immediate turn round, and returned home with his cargo in about five months, to sail into Texel on 31 May 1755.

This time it was eighteen months before he was appointed to another ship, and ordered to another destination – Bengal. As captain of the *Bronstee*, he had a rise in pay from 72 to 80 guilders a month, his greater experience obviously justifying such an increase. He needed it, too. He made the outward voyage in eight months and when he returned, probably early in 1758, he was greeted with the latest addition to his family, another daughter. She seems to have been born not long after his departure, for she was christened Johanna Cornelia by a pastor of Amsterdam's Lutheran church on 27 April 1757.

Bengal was his destination once more on his next voyage, which was exceptionally long. Sailing from Texel on 5 December 1759, the *'t Huys te Manpad* did not reach her destination until 9 January 1761, with twenty-five of her crew of 238 dying on the voyage. Possibly the ship was in some way defective, or one of those which got a reputation as being 'unlucky' for, although she had been built in Amsterdam only in 1745, the Company sold her in 1766. For the return trip, Klump was transferred to *de Snoek* (the 'Pike'), named after the fish, so common in Cape waters, which gained such an unhappy reputation in the Britain of the Second World War when it was promoted as a substitute for tinned salmon. This vessel belonged to the Zeeland Chamber of the Dutch East India Company, and this time Klump tied up at the Zeeland mooring at Rammekens when he returned to Holland on 29 June 1762. On board he had his own cargo of linen which he had bought at Batavia for 15,396 roepias, and which he would no doubt sell in Amsterdam for a handsome profit.

It was the profit from such private trade that enabled Willem Klump to retire from the sea fourteen years after the loss of the *Amsterdam*, and set himself up in business ashore. This plan was linked with the marriage of his eldest daughter Elysabet to a distant relative, Christoffel Hendrik Klump, which took place on 29 July 1762, only four weeks after *de Snoek* had docked. His son-in-law had been born, like himself, at Mittau on the eastern Baltic coast, and just before the wedding, on 23 July 1762, they entered into partnership to trade in wine. Willem put up 25,000 guilders, and Christoffel 10,000, and it is an indication of how the business prospered that in 1764 Willem was able to buy a house for 13,500 guilders. It overlooked a canal, but was later demolished and a modern building now stands on the site at 860 Prinsengracht.

The joint will made by Willem and Margareta on 25 July 1769, however, reveals that his later life was troubled. Provision was made for their second daughter, Anna, now sixteen, who was described as their 'unhealthy and imbecile daughter', and she was apparently in nursing care in, or near, Huizen, a small town to the east of Amsterdam. Her illness must have overshadowed the marriage on 9 February 1770 of the couple's eldest son, Coenraad, to Sara Carelson, the illegitimate daughter of Willem's half-brother Frans. The latter was a wealthy merchant, living on the Keizersgracht, and had long ago agreed to be the guardian of Willem's children should Margareta die while her husband was at sea.

Less than five weeks after the wedding, Anna died, and on 16 March Willem purchased the grave in the Dutch Reformed church at Huizen where she was buried three days later. It seems that Willem and Margareta could not have found much comfort in each other at this time, for in June 1770, despite his wife's legitimate claim on his eventual estate, he made a new will totally excluding her. The new beneficiaries were his children and grandchildren, among whom he divided his money and most treasured possessions, including a gold watch with an embossed case; but his silver-hilted sword and diamond cuff-links were bequeathed to his son-in-law Christoffel.

Four months later Willem made another will in which Margareta was still excluded, but was at least appointed an executor. By July 1771 the marital rift seems to have been healed, for in yet another will, Margareta is the chief beneficiary if she should survive her husband. There is evidence now, however, of another family disagreement, for Elysabet's inheritance was reduced from a sum of money to the interest on some invested capital, though her little son Willem, was obviously still in favour with his grandfather, for he was to inherit all his clothing, as well as his fine gold and silver possessions.

The reason seems to have been that Willem was by now in financial difficulty, and had embezzled funds from the family business. Elysabet's husband, Christoffel, suspected what was happening and, as partner, took legal steps when his father-in-law refused to allow him to examine the accounts. Willem tried, presumably as senior partner, to obtain legal backing for his refusal to 'open the books', but his failure would seem to be reflected in his payment to Christoffel on 9 December 1773 of 1,300 guilders in settlement of his interest in their 'trade in wine and strong drink'. The business itself seems to have come to an end some time in 1772 or 1773.

Willem's financial troubles evidently grew worse, for on 12 July 1775 he sold his home for 12,000 guilders and died three months later aged only sixty. He was buried on 14 October 1775 in his daughter's grave in the church at Huizen, though for some unknown reason both bodies were transferred on 9 June 1779 to grave forty-one in the choir of the church. At his death the cash from the house sale meant that Willem was taxed as a first class person.

Margareta moved to a house on Herengracht, near the Gast-huismolensteeg, again overlooking a canal, and the next year her nineteen-year-old daughter Johanna married a doctor, Wolter Forsten Verschuur. Possibly Margareta had further financial troubles, or perhaps dowered her daughter well, for by the time she also was laid to rest in 1781, in the same grave as her husband and Anna in the brick church at Huizen, she was taxed as a poor fourth class person.

And there the Klump story might have ended, had not Ken Wilkie, formerly of *Holland Herald*, decided to search the National Genealogical Archive at the Hague for some record of Willem's children. All he could find was that Johanna Klump's death had been registered at Groningen in 1838. She and her husband had had two daughters, the eldest being Johanna Cornelia Forstein Verschuur, who had married a Nicolaas Johannes Diderik de Fremery. Their direct descendants have now been located living at The Hague, in Rotterdam and in Australia. Touchingly, it has also been discovered that Johanna Klump and her husband exchanged gifts at their wedding, a pair of cups and saucers, each carrying a silhouette of the other partner in the marriage, and that these survive. We have no likeness of Willem Klump, but at least the silhouette of his daughter, now carefully preserved in Australia, helps to bridge the gap of two centuries.

All this detailed research allows us to build up a very lively impression of the captain of the *Amsterdam*. No idealistic hero, he was a Company man who put the safety of his ship and cargo before that of his dying crew, and was prepared to renege on his promise (certainly extracted under duress) to pay those still on their feet to save the ship's treasure. His flouting of the Company rules on private trade was the common practice of Company officials, and even the Company winked at it.

In both business and personal relationships he seems to have been rather impetuous, and even domineering and insensitive at times. Yet, there are hints of a warm heart in those bequests to his little grandson, and in the fact that his marriage did, despite difficulties, endure. There was a dash of style, too, in a man who sported diamond cuff-links and that sword with the silver hilt. In fact, regarding him as a probably typical sea captain of his time, we can better understand the clash of interests and personality between him and his crew, which formed such an important element in the mutiny which led to the sinking of the ship on the beach at Hastings.

Unlike some of the crew of the *Amsterdam*, Klump had at least a full and prosperous spell of working life ahead of him after the wrecking of his ship and in that he was also more fortunate than his most important passengers. Andries van Bockom and Pieternella returned to the Netherlands from Hastings, and were assigned fresh passenger places in the *Sloterdijk* under the command of Captain Lieutenant Harmanus Soet. They sailed from Texel on 30 September 1749, reached the Cape for a three-week spell of revictualling, and arrived at Batavia uneventfully on 4 May 1750, a fairly average journey. Van Bockom was then posted to Malaya, where he became a Harbour-master or *sabandhaar*, and Secretary of Police, but in October 1759

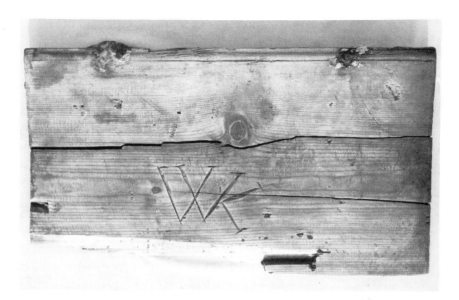

VII. The lid of a chest bearing the initials WK (above), showing that it must have belonged to Captain Willem Klump, was probably from one of the five chests of wine bottles listed under his name in the Paybook. The cup and saucer (below), bearing the silhouette of his daughter, Johanna Klump, was presumably given to her husband at their marriage. It is in the keeping of one of their descendants in Australia.

he died, still only thirty-six, possibly from some tropical disease. Pieternella survived, and after the usualy delays, her widow's settlement was approved by the Company on 28 April 1762. It seems likely that she had by then returned home.

We don't know whether her younger sister Catharina was still with her to comfort her, and it doesn't even appear whether she ventured on that second voyage to the East at all after the *Amsterdam* disaster. Like Englishwomen who went out to India under the raj, Dutch ladies who went out to the Company stations were usually intending to marry, if not accompanying or joining their husbands. Yet we find that in a testament by her father dated 4 March 1760, when she was thirty-four, she is referred to as unmarried. Perhaps she was disappointed in love. The chances of our finding out would in most similar instances seem small, but perhaps there are descendants of other members of the Van Bockom and Schook families who may know: Pieternella and her husband would seem to have had no children.

As for the other passengers, we find that military lieutenant Jacob Hal was so anxious to continue his voyage to the Indies that he did not want to return to Amsterdam to take the next ship from there, but asked the VOC directors for permission to travel out in one of the sister ships of the *Amsterdam*'s fleet which were sheltering in English ports, probably Portsmouth. This attempt to save time failed, and his transfer took so long to arrange that the ships sailed without him and he and his wife were granted leave to join the *Overness* on 14 April 1749, which did not sail until the following July from Holland. Curiously enough, passage was also provided this time for a maid for his wife, and although only their haste to depart may have prevented her having one when they first set out, it is an amusing speculation that Maria Monk could have taken up this idea from seeing Pieternella Bockom-Schook, who had had her sister with her in this capacity. She may have decided that, if she were shipwrecked again, she would at least do so with the right degree of style to impress the inhabitants when rescued!

Style, however, is a relative term, and it is by no means the least of the attractions of the *Amsterdam* that no one aboard her was highly born. Her passengers and officers were not titled people, and, together with her crew and complement of soldiers, represent the ordinary folk who were the backbone of early Dutch society and trade. But for the discovery of the ship, no one would have troubled to trace the interweavings of human lives in Amsterdam which led to the cast of characters present at that dramatic moment of the wreck, but now it is assured that research will follow every name in the vessel's paybook. For years to come it will be a continuing story, and the vision of the Dutch merchants who accepted the challenge of their expanding world and the concept of a global trade, will take flesh in the details we shall learn of the people aboard the *Amsterdam* who played their part in making it come true.

7

Legends and Plunder

In the years following the loss of the *Amsterdam* only a few connoisseurs of the curious and the fishermen whose nets were snagged by the jagged timbers just above the seabed ever gave a thought to the lost ship. Among them her story was handed down by word of mouth, becoming embellished and distorted in the retelling, so that fiction took the place of fact.

By the nineteenth century Hastings had begun to take on a new role as one of the newly popular seaside resorts; and, ideally situated as it was a little more than an hour's distance from London when the railway was established, a mass tourist traffic began. Much of old Hastings was submerged by hotels and boarding houses, and surrounding land also gave birth to rows of terraced Victorian residences, narrow fronted, with iron railings defending their basement kitchens, and stairs rising four, five and six storeys to make one wonder at the endurance of the holidaymakers, and still more the 'slaveys' who toiled up and down serving their needs. So great was the influx that a new town to the west – St Leonards – was established to cater for the more select visitor, and the atmosphere still subtly changes as one passes the stone monument on the sea front which is the only actual boundary between the two.

The nineteenth-century newcomers brought work for others, but were incredibly leisured themselves. They arrived with their nursemaids and their personal maids, and a paraphernalia of trunks, and stayed for substantial periods, establishing themselves with library subscriptions and attending churches of thier own particular denomination. They needed guidebooks which would supply such practical information for day-to-day living in their temporarily adopted town, and they also wanted to know about local beauty spots to be seen and something of the historical background of their chosen resort. Local guides poured from the presses and although some were good, and others were bad, most were an amalgam of material copied from their predecessors. Hastings public library has a large collection, and each has its own version of Hastings history, including the incident of the *Amsterdam*.

The earliest, of particular interest and value because it was written almost within living memory of the loss of the ship, appeared in 1808. In the section headed Bulverhithe – the modern spelling is Bulverhythe – we find:

'Upon the sands of this place are the remains of a remarkable large Dutch ship called the *Amsterdam*, the ribs of which, after a boisterous sea washes the sand away, are to be seen enitre and disclose nearly its circumference, sometimes apearing four or five feet above the sands. It is supposed to have been run ashore about seventy years ago by convicts, who had mutinied, and was loaded with treasure some of which according to report, found its way to Hastings, and enriched several of its honest inhabitants.

'The ship being of immense weight, as may be seen by the timbers of it, and most of the cargo ponderous commodities was soon enveloped in the sands, and all attempts to clear the lower deck, even with the assistance of soldiers quartered in the neighbourhood, proved abortive, in consequence of the tide returning before it could be effected: and the greatest part of the hull now remains a monument to the power of the raging ocean. Many of the crew were drowned, and brought to Hastings to be buried.

Half-truth, fact and fiction were nicely mingled.

Probably two years later than this guidebook account we come to a curious little document, written in ink upon a small sheet of now yellowed paper, which is preserved in Hastings Museum.

'To the incredulous is presented

A piece of the Amsterdam East Indiaman wrecked 60 years ago in Pevensey Bay at a place called Bulverhithe between Bexhill & Hastings supposed to be laden with copper or other valuable metal to recover wch two hund. German legion have been employed to dig her up.

> George Norman
> John Fuller Mrs.
> George Ward Norman
> Charlotte Norman
> Charlotte Norman Junr
> Thomas Shorter   *Mayor*
> Edward Milward   *Principal Inhabitant*
> John Phillips   *Smuggler*
> Hastings, April 27th

The above piece of wood was cut off the wreck by one of Mr Norman's servants April 22nd 1808.'

83

A piece of wood is glued to the paper, and from the differing hands of the signatures, it seems likely that the basic document is authentic, but the pencilled notes (indicated here by italics) would seem of later date, since they include two errors. Thomas Shorter was never Mayor of Hastings, whereas Edward Milward – listed as the 'principal inhabitant' – was the actual holder of the office in 1808. And, as we know from other sources, the German legion who dug into the ship carried out their operations in 1810 not 1808.

Another curious item is an eye-witness account of the wreck published in an 'old newspaper' of 1837, now untraceable, but which was reproduced elsewhere in 1867 and 1880. The original is quoted as saying that 'an old man, now 97 years of age, remembers the circumstance and his testimony is highly interesting' – which indicates that the old gentleman was a boy of eight when the event actually took place. The account goes on: 'This ship was 997 tons burthen, 151 feet long and 39 feet wide across the beam. She had a general cargo of cutlery, glass and china, about ten tons of copper, and a quantity of quicksilver, and two or three cases of specie. She also mounted 14 guns. This valuable ship was run ashore on a Sunday morning in the year 1749 by a crew that had mutinied, in consequence, as it is said, of having plague on board.' The old fellow went on to add the interesting detail that the Dutch vessel was run ashore into muddy ground covered with sedges and weeds, which is the only indication we have as to the state of the sea bottom at the time of the wreck.

Despite some inaccuracy as to detail – for example, the Amsterdam had 54 guns not 14, and we know that she had 28 cases of silver, not 2 or 3 – the account would seem to be a genuine first-hand recollection. Not only does the narrator give the right year for the wreck, at a time when the date was generally unknown, but he knows that it took place on a Sunday. These points help to give weight to his reference to a mutiny, which accords with the evidence in that direction mentioned in earlier chapters, and that the deaths on board were caused by some kind of virulent disease, perhaps the plague.

This newspaper account, however, does not seem to have reached a very wide readership and the guidebooks went on giving dates ranging from 1742 to 1769 for the wreck. It was not until the discovery of the Collier letters at the end of the nineteenth century that the true date was authoritatively established.

Meanwhile, the *Amsterdam* legend was further embroidered. An account of 1835 attributes the cause of the wreck to the ship having been run ashore in fog, and gives a date of 1755. *Brett's Gazette* in 1879 has an article by a man whose aunt 'used to say that her uncle, Richard Roffe, who bequeathed a large amount of property to his nieces and other persons, was credited with bringing home from the *Amsterdam* a quantity of money in his long-legged leather boots'. At first sight, this suggested that Roffe was one of Anthony Watson's accomplices, but further research showed that at the date of the wreck Roffe was only three years old. The article concludes, therefore, that it must have been the great-uncle of that name 'who thus made his long leather boots a pair of strong money bags on that occasion.'

From 1837 onwards reference to a 'plague' or 'fever' is a recurrent feature in all accounts. Particularly interesting on this score is the account given by J. Lucas, a local student of history, who seems to have been collecting material for possible publication (now preserved in the special file in Hastings library), although his book or article never materialised. In 1911 he questioned various people in order to record tradition before it was forgotten, and wrote in May that 'several fishermen have told me, at different times and places, and quite independently of each other, that at the time of the wreck of the *Amsterdam* there was yellow fever on board; and that it was on this account that no efforts were made for a long time to recover the cargo; but two old men corrected me repeatedly when I told them this, saying that it was black fever'.

As has been seen, this insistence on the presence of fever seems to have been a true reflection of the events of 1749. Our local historian was indefatigable in collecting all the information he could, realising that by 1911 it was the last chance to collect anything of value, and he fortunately wrote it all down, not attempting to sift it on the basis of the inadequate existing evidence. One man he questioned was one of the family which produced *Brett's Gazette*, quoted above. 'Mr Brett,' he records, 'aged 62, told me that his grandfather, who was born in 1785, always said that none of the crew were drowned, but that several of them came ashore with yellow fever on them, and wandered away and died in the woods, where they were found by the "long dogs" [greyhounds].' In March 1971 I, too, had personal experience of the survival of this story in oral tradition when I met a man who had lived close to Bulverhythe all his life and well remembered playing in the wreck as a small boy. It was clear that he knew nothing of the guidebooks in Hastings library, yet he, and his parents and local friends, were all conversant with the story of the fever.

Another detail on which people have fastened ever since the wreck is the shifting of the sands at the site. The same Bulverhythe man described to me how greatly the beach changes with the seasons and state of the weather. I have myself observed how the gales and rough seas of the winter tend to scour shallow hollows in the beach around the wreck, which are filled with sand in the comparative calm of summer. Once I saw the whole after part of the ship buried, and, after a severe gale in January 1974, the entire vessel was covered by sand. Usually, however, the forward end projects about a metre from the beach, and the rest of the vessel has a gradual slope, so that the stern is level with the shore. The port quarter is always buried beneath a bank of sand.

During the winter of 1878–9, however, there was a highly abnormal change. About two feet of sand was scoured away from the site, so that when exceptionally low spring tides also occurred in March of 1879, the bow stood out five feet high and the midships part as much as three feet, so that the wreck was visible from a mile away during the whole of the week. The scoured beach gradually filled again with sand, but such a happening, rare though it was, does make it seem strange that so few attempts at salvage were made, when it was common knowledge that so little of the cargo had been recovered at the time of the actual wreck.

Very probably individuals did make desultory attempts of which we have no record, but the sand being completely saturated, any hole made in the ship fills at once with mingled water and sand, making it impossible to get deeper than six feet simply by using a shovel. Add to this the fact that the tide remains at the right level only for a few brief hours on just a few days a year, and the lack of success of any such attempts becomes less surprising. For any treasure-hunting to have a chance of success needed a determined and comparatively scientific attack by a substantial number of men.

The first serious salvage attempt on these lines was made in 1810 by two hundred men of George III's German Legion, who were stationed in nearby Bexhill. Their commanding officer, Colonel Halkett, gave them permission to dig into the ship for copper and anything else they might find. Even two hundred men, however, found that they got nowhere before the returning tide frustrated them – fortunately for us.

The next attempt was made by several out-of-work labourers, also from Bexhill. Starting to dig inside the bow of the ship on Monday, 19 February 1827, they managed to reach the orlop deck by the low tide of Wednesday. Clearly they were digging through a pre-existent hole in the lower deck at the bow made by the salvors of 1749, and they must have used wooden shuttering to retain the loose sides of the hole as they worked. They broke into the boatswain's store, and discovered 'a large cask, containing one thousand knives, mostly in a corroded state, with black wooden handles'.

VIII. The tobacco box from the *Amsterdam* found during the nineteenth century. On the lid (above) an old man sits on a stool rocking a baby in a cradle while his wife clandestinely meets her lover in another room (to the right); freely rendered, the inscription reads: 'How can a young wife deceive her old husband? Another man made the child and he has to rock the cradle.' On the base the decoration shows one of the famous brothels of Amsterdam. To the left, a man and woman are drinking at a bar (the inscription reading: 'At the front I drink'); to the right is a large bed in a rear room, the inscription reading: 'At the back I sleep'. Some censorious hand has attempted to scratch out the couple in the bed.

Further finds included glass, beads, pottery, goblets and wine glasses, as well as mysterious square glass bottles 'figured in gold', which seems to be a reference to the iridescence, due to corrosion, which gives such colour to archaeological finds of glass. Similar 'gold' coloured glass was found in 1984. A whetstone for sharpening knives also turned up, and could even be ascribed to an owner, since it bore the name of 'Iohan C. van Hacke', and the date '10 Sept. 1745'. Johan Haake of Braakwe was one of the soldiers aboard the *Amsterdam*.

The Bexhill men were delighted and hastened to put their treasures on the market, where the current taste for antiquities ensured that they 'fetched a great price', which in turn ensured that the Lord Warden of the Cinque Ports was stirred to take an interest. All wrecks on this strech of coast were the charge of this official, whose post went back into the mists of the Middle Ages and who was technically still bound to co-ordinate the efforts of the five major ports to supply men and ships to face invaders. A claim was now made on his behalf for the salvaged goods still in the men's possession, and the income from those which had been sold, and further salvage was only to be allowed on terms which rendered it unprofitable to the enterprising labourers of Bexhill. They were disappointed and understandably embittered, and a contemporary account ends with the comment, 'and there the wreck lies – a representation of the fable of the dog in the manger'.

We don't know what were the exact terms proposed at this period, but during the Duke of Wellington's tenure of the wardenship, someone else wanted to obtain official permission to dig, and we have a letter written by His Grace detailing them, and there seems no reason to think that they differed from those offered to the Bexhill men. Any goods valued at less than £100 in any one year were to be the property of the salvor, but anything in excess of this would entitle the Lord Warden to deduct his percentage. Curiously, the percentage is not given, but we can be glad that it was apparently sufficiently high to ensure that the wreck remained undisturbed by this most successful of all the early salvage teams.

The next attempt was more high-sounding in that the group of people concerned formed a company for the purpose, but although they found 'several articles of foreign manufacture which were afterwards sold as curiosities', they had very little significant success in their dig of 20 April 1827. Ten years later, on 3 April 1837, yet another and even less successful try is reported, but with no finds at all being made.

For more than a century all organised excavation now ceased, and only desultory finds of the most casual nature are recorded. A local fisherman

X. Objects recovered from the orlop deck, among the stores at the bow, include brushes of eather (upper left), a small keg of tallow (upper right), and pulley blocks of various sizes elow). The deadeye (below, far left) is from the foremast 'channel' on the port side of the ship.

acquired a 'hand-bill' and other things before May 1911, and another man had a chopper. Someone else had the good luck to come across a pewter spoon, now in Hastings Museum, and an undecorated glass cup which long ago disappeared, although there is a surviving photograph. Two similar glass cups, however, both decorated, a wine glass, and a decorated and inscribed brass tobacco box, whose discoverers are unknown, did find their way to the Museum where they still remain.

No one seems to have drawn or painted the *Amsterdam* in the time of the craze for the romantic and picturesque – perhaps there wasn't quite enough visible to 'compose' the right sort of picture – and we have to wait for photography to give us an actual impression of the scene in earlier days. The first known photographs were taken in March 1908, and more on 13 May 1911 at six o'clock in the evening. Apart from some erosion of the timbers, these show the wreck much as it is now, the only change being some damage done by the salvage work of 1969. More photographs were taken by Mr C. Parsons while on holiday about 1961, and I am grateful to him for sending them to me.

By 1936 or 1937 the story of the *Amsterdam* once again took a more criminal turn. A local confidence trickster approached some of the more substantial citizens of Hastings with the suggestion that they contribute £100 to enable a salvage scheme to be undertaken. It was an excellent scheme, in view of surviving memories of treasure and a valuable cargo, though the trickster had no intention of ever recovering the ship's valuables, for once he had acquired some contributions he intended to disappear. John Manwaring Baines, curator of Hastings Museum, to whom I am indebted for this story, kindly wrote me a full account, and added: 'having no money to spare myself – certainly not £100 – I paid no particular attention to it, but I do recall it's being mentioned on quite a number of occasions. I do not remember any prosecutions, however.'

And so the *Amsterdam* rested as a half-forgotten memory until suddenly in August 1969 she hit the headlines with reports and photographs of a mass of newly-discovered antiquities. They had been brought to light by workmen in the employ of a contractor, William Press & Son Ltd., completing a new main sewer about a quarter of a mile away from the actual site.

Jack Aaron, the firms' chief diver, visited Hastings Museum and noticed some of the objects from the wreck on display. The labelling referred him to the book, *Historic Hastings*, by John Manwaring Baines for further details, and he found in the appendix to the book extracts from the Collier letters

X. Two of the bronze smoothing irons with broken handles (above), recovered in 1969, showing the compartments for red-hot charcoal in their bases; and (below) two of the fine bronze candlesticks of slightly differing design found in 1969, with the damaged remains of others.

describing the circumstances of the wreck. He showed these and the photograph of the remains of the ship which the book also contained, to Ken Young, the site agent on the outfall scheme, who was a local man with a keen sense of history, and so already knew something of the ship. Since they had a mechanical excavator at hand, they decided to dig into the wreck at the next low tides, and see what they could find. On 31 July the great lumbering machine on its crawler tracks followed the receding tide through the shingle of the storm beach down to the almost flat stretch of sand which lies beyond. Moving into position beside the bow of the wreck, the driver of the excavator started plunging its great shovel into the sand, digging deeper and deeper. The sides of the waterlogged hole soon began slumping in, and the gathering spectators could see only a hollow filled with a soup-like mingle of water and sand. At about 5 metres down, the shovel began to bring up through this mess objects – brushes made of heather, staves of barrels, pulley blocks of various sizes, and a beautifully carved wooden shoe last. As the shovelfuls were dumped onto the beach outside the wreck area, the sightseers began raking through the slime in which everything below the upper sand level is embedded, and which has a most putrid smell.

A race began between the workmen and the newcomers as to who would get the best objects first. A visitor who began walking off with a perfectly-preserved wooden pulley block, only changed his mind when surrounded by several hefty members of the party with the prior claim, and a shoe-last which was unwarily put down after its legitimate finders had examined it disappeared for good. There was even a four-footed diespoiler on the track, for when the excavator smashed into a barrel of tallow and scattered the pieces on the beach, a dog out for an evening stroll with its owner sampled it with apparent relish, everyone being too surprised to drive it away in time. The dog was not seen again, but assuming that the consumption of tallow is not in itself fatal, the preservative quality of the setting in which it was discovered would make it no more indigestible now than when the wreck first happened. Meanwhile, chaos reigned as the hectic scramble for souvenirs continued until the tide returned after a little over two hours. A photograph taken the next morning shows the beach around the *Amsterdam* littered with uncollected antiquities washed out by the action of the waves as the sea covered the ship again during the night.

Spurred on by their success, the workmen decided to dig into another part of the wreck on the next day, and chose the area amidships where the tops of two transverse rows of wooden posts were normally visible. The excavator smashed through some of the posts on the port side and dug down and down, dumping the excavated material, which included substantial pieces of the ship's structure onto the beach. At a depth of about 2.5 metres the excavator suddenly hit a hard surface – the lower gun deck – and amidst the sand and water soup filling the hole, the necks of dozens of glass bottles suddenly popped up. They were full wine bottles, and the indiscriminate energy of the excavator ensured that many broke and red wine mingled its stain freely with the sandy salt water.

While some of the workmen excitedly collected as many of the whole bottles as they could, others paused to uncork a few, and to smell and even to taste the liquid. Its bouquet was somewhat strong and the taste foul, but scientific examination later helped to prove that the view of the finders that the wine had been heavily contaminated with sewage was incorrect. Yet others among the workmen were doing their best to fend off the growing crowd of holidaymakers and local people who were bent on further souvenirs. The scene of the previous day was well on its way to repetition, and it was not difficult to visualise the clash which developed between the troops and the local 'beachcombers' in just such a way in the weeks following the original wreck. In the general hubbub the number of bottles recovered was not noted, although estimates range from sixty to eighty, and the lorry on which they were placed was not guarded. The result was that many more disappeared, even though the local Customs and Excise officer was present, and the sum total of full bottles reaching safe custody in Hastings Museum was five!

A degree of calm having been restored, the excavator once more went into action in the same area, and within minutes brought up the most valuable prizes yet recovered – five exceptionally well-preserved bronze cannon, each bearing the insignia of the Amsterdam Chamber of the Dutch East India Company and the date 1748. According to the discoverers, each cannon originally had traces of the sacking in which it had been wrapped as part of the ship's cargo, and although this was destroyed when the pieces were cleaned, Ken Young did manage to find for me a fragment of the black concretion which had formed around them as they lay buried, and which retained a clear cast of the texture of the sacking. Other finds in the hole included stoneware bottles from the Rhine region, probably containing gin before the excavator smashed them, and at least one soldier's belt to which were attached a bronze cartridge case and a bronze pricker for clearing the touch hole of a musket.

Finally, during subsequent low tides, the digging was moved to the stern and here two excavators working simultaneously found the bulk of the smaller objects recovered in 1969. These apparently included brass pins, pewter spoons, bronze candlesticks, smoothing irons, cooking pots, and sticks of sealing wax. It was a remarkable collection in which about three quarters of the items were smashed or damaged by the mechanical excavator's clumsiness. As a reminder of the very real human tragedy this ship represents, some human bones were also brought up. All of these artefacts, as well as the bones, which proved to be those of Adrian Welgevaren, came from the lower gun deck of the *Amsterdam*, but how much damage the hull structure actually suffered was then not quite clear, but was only revealed in the archaeological excavation of 1984. This showed that although deck planks and beams had been torn up and many objects had been smashed, the main hull structure remained intact and, even on the lower gun deck, there was a substantial area of undisturbed objects left where they had been abandoned in 1749.

Towards the very end of the treasure hunt, the excavators were moved outside the wreck, and tried digging there. One rapidly found what was thought to be the fallen main mast on the west side of the wreck, and instead of clearing the sand above in order to examine it, the operator locked his shovel round the end and heaved. It is reported that the beach heaved upward for about fifty feet (15.2 metres) from this point, and continuous pressure was applied until the mast snapped, and was left with its end angled out of the sand. Some excavation was also done alongside the ship, when about six lower dead-eyes (pierced wooden blocks linking the ropes which steadied the mast) were found, each still apparently attached to the side of the ship by its chain plate, and each still containing part of the lanyard by which it was originally connected to the upper deadeyes.

The salvaged objects were now handed over to the Receiver of Wreck, together with a formal claim for a salvage award, and he allowed the bulk of them to be temporarily stowed away at Hastings Museum while they awaited due process of the law. It was to be a long wait of several years.

It was at this stage that the solicitor acting for William Press & Son Ltd., contacted several members of the Council for Nautical Archaeology (as it is now known), including myself, as I had investigated several old shipwreck sites. He felt, as did the men who had been working on the wreck, that it might have an archaeological value, and a meeting was held in his London office. Among those present were representatives of the contractors, including Ken Young; and of the CNA, including Basil Bathe, Keeper of the Department of Ships at the Science Museum and Lt.-Cdr. Alan Bax, a very active diver with a keen interest in nautical archaeology. Ken outlined what had been done and the nature of the finds, but when he explained that he and his colleagues believed a very considerable part of the ship and her contents still remained intact in the beach, I confessed I reserved judgment. It was too good to be true. Such a thing might happen, but the chances against it were astronomical, and as an archaeologist working on London building sites, I had grown sceptical of the strange stories told and the rash assumptions made by well-intentioned people with no archaeological experience.

Nevertheless, there was something strangely compelling about the *Amsterdam*. At the time of the meeting, however, when the representatives of William Press put it squarely to us that we were being invited to take over subsequent salvage of the wreck, if we felt that it had sufficient archaeological value, it was not an easy decision to make. The ship would be visible once again, they told us, during the last week in September. This meant that there was little over a month to prepare for some sort of initial survey.

I well remember the pause that followed, as they ended putting their case. How could we take on the *Amsterdam*, even if she were the ideal archaeological site, I told myself she very probably was not? There was absolutely no money, no staff, no equipment, no archaeological museum facilities, and all work would have to be carried out during holiday leave, and in other moments of scanty leisure. On top of this, there would be undoubted problems consequent upon the need to undertake this highly specialised archaeological task within the framework of a law of salvage designed to meet purely commercial needs. Finally, we did not know the owners of the ship, nor what restrictions they might place on our activities should we succeed in discovering who they might be. Was it worth it? All these daunting considerations rushed through my mind during that pause – and in face of such an opportunity, each and every one was inadequate. Besides, as the only archaeologist there with experience of investigating shipwrecks, the decision was really mine and how could such a challenge be resisted? Success could only be achieved by building up a team, but with men such as Alan Bax to count on, the beginnings of it were already there. I accepted . . .

8

Planning

The kind of archaeological work we were about to undertake on the *Amsterdam* was unique. There had never been any other investigation of a well-preserved wreck of a large historic ship buried in a narrow inter-tidal zone, so that we had to devise special techniques.

It would have been easiest to use divers, in the sense that we could then have worked, weather allowing, at any time during the larger part of the year, but this method would also have brought its own difficulties, the one which weighed most with me being the danger of misinterpretation of archaeological features which had not been properly seen. I felt that, with careful planning, we would be able to discover what we needed to know in the two hours, rarely more, that the lowest tides would give us in the few days of certain months each year. I used the few weeks till the next occasion they occurred in establishing a research programme. Although prevented by existing commitments in London from obtaining any preview of the wreck before the actual investigation started, I was able to get a good impression of the situation by examining the many photographs which had now been taken, and discussed with Ken Young the difficulties we should be up against.

Particularly difficult was the making of any accurate judgement as to how far the ship had sunk into the beach. An obvious clue was the partly surviving head of the ship at the bow, just projecting above the sand, and even more useful was Ken Young's observation that there were apparently traces of gunports roughly at beach level. One of the many photographs he showed me did, in fact, show what could only be the lower half of a gunport, and below it part of a deck. Nobody could remember the precise point at which the photograph had been taken, but it seemed to be a little forward of

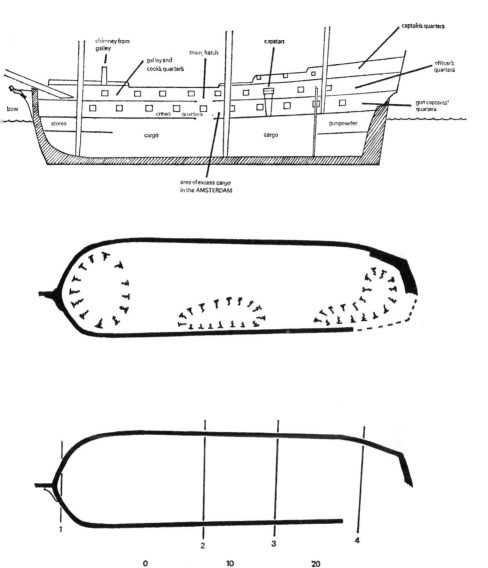

5. A reconstruction of an East Indiaman such as the *Amsterdam* in long section (above), showing where the main stowage compartments and quarters lay; (centre) the areas of the *Amsterdam* excavated by the workmen of William Press Ltd in 1969, when they dug into the ship and recovered many antiquities; and (below) the position of the probed profiles of the ship (profiles 1–4), see also p. 116.

the stern on the port side.

This was remarkably heartening in itself, but it was also a reminder that it was time for me to take a lesson or two in the detailed anatomy of eighteenth-century Dutch East Indiamen. It was not a branch of knowledge of which I had previously found much need in my work at the Guildhall Museum in the City of London, and the Roman and medieval ships, which I had encountered in the bed of the Thames, were not really comparable.

The first obvious source of information was the National Maritime Museum's collection of paintings and illustrated books, which supplied a beautiful assortment of these splendid vessels. They were of considerable help, but the artists, careful as to external detail as they were, naturally concentrated on showing the ships as sailing vessels. There seemed to be no artist, and in view of the Dutch love of land interiors one might have expected at least one or two, who had painted scenes below deck. The Museum's reserve collection, however, included another most valuable source of information in a beautiful model of an early eighteenth-century Indiaman, the *Seven Provinces*. Obviously there must have been design changes between the date of this ship and the building of the *Amsterdam*, but her general lines were the same. Her two main gun decks were especially interesting, for it seemed that the gunport which Ken Young had seen in our ship must belong either to the upper or lower of these, since the forecastle, quarter and poop decks had undoubtedly been destroyed.

Of course all this needed checking, but it provided a useful preliminary hypothesis. Our first task must be to find out which of the two gun decks we had to deal with, for upon this would depend not only interpretation of any other features which we may discover, but also the whole research programme. This could easily be done by using an excavator to dig a hole outside the ship, for we should then see whether or not a second row of gunports lay beneath the first, and know at once whether the wreck was complete merely from the lower deck, or from the upper gun deck – a much more exciting prospect. It was clear that at least nothing higher than the upper gun deck could survive, since the gunport which had been seen at the stern could not have belonged to the quarter deck. Had it been part of this, there would have been well defined traces of the ship's waist in the middle of the outline of the wreck, between the quarter deck itself and the forecastle.

Alan Bax kindly agreed to go down to Hastings on my behalf at the end of August, and Ken Young promised to dig us the necessary hole. I envied Alan his first contact with the wreck, and was glad to lunch with him in the City as soon as he returned in order to hear his news. Eagerly he reported that he had seen, about two metres down in the sand, one gunport of the second row belonging to the lower deck. We could now be reasonably sure that this great ship had survived, not only up to, but partly above her upper gun deck: she was approximately two thirds complete!

In view of the quality of the find, and the value of the information we hoped to obtain from her, it was obvious that work on her was a job for experts and the team must remain small. I was very fortunate in the calibre of the people who came forward to help, and who gave of their best in what was to be a long, tiring investigation, and who did so entirely at their own expense. Throughout the story the right people, with the right skills, always seemed to be available at the right time to deal with the specific aspects and problems which lay in their particular fields.

Bill St John Wilkes, and his wife Ann, were the first of them, and were untiring in their efforts and the mainstay of our work on the site. Since he lived at nearby Eastbourne, and was a member of the Council for Nautical Archaeology, Bill had already made a point of meeting Ken Young, even before he knew of my own involvement in the *Amsterdam*. As soon as he heard that I had taken charge of the investigation, he wrote an enthusiastic offer of help, and was able to give some useful suggestions on coping with some of the unusual problems presented by the site.

John Manwaring Baines was particularly glad that we were assuming responsibility for the *Amsterdam*. Without assistants at Hastings Museum and with a limited budget, which made no allowance for any archaeological research, he regretted deeply his inability to help us more, but the role he and Hastings Town Council were to play was nevertheless an important one.

The final member of the team, whose presence was to assure the eventual success of the investigation, was a corporate body – the British Broadcasting Corporation. Paul Johnstone, the executive producer of their television programme *Chronicle*, decided to make a full-length feature of our work, after George Naish had mentioned to him what we planned to do. Sensing an interesting story, Paul handed the task to one of his production team, Ray Sutcliffe, who had a personal and active interest in historic ships and archaeology, and both proved to be yet other examples of the right person at the right time. The BBC film made possible many aspects of the investigation which could not have been otherwise undertaken on our non-existent budget.

Even on the most economical basis, I had estimated that we needed £500, and applied to many sources in a constant search for funds: lack of financial support was a serious problem at all stages. The Department of

Trade and Industry, which administered the law relating to the salvage of wrecked ships on behalf of the Government, and which might have been expected to take an interest, replied that it had no provision for dealing with archaeological sites. As far as they were concerned there was in law no such thing as an historic wreck, and they advised me to contact the Ancient Monuments section of the Department of the Environment, which administers the law, and Government funds, in respect of archaeological sites.

The Ancient Monuments division sent my problem to their lawyers, having never encountered anything like this before, and they, too, decided in their wisdom that they could not be held responsible for any archaeological sites which happened to be below high water mark. This apparently rendered us quite ineligible for any sort of grant. I applied to various other possible sources without success, and in the end the only money grant received for the work was £25 from Hastings Museum, although much later on, when the matter had been drawn to the attention of the Dutch Government and they had established their claim as owners of the ship, they gave a grant which enabled me to visit the Netherlands to study material in the archives and museums there.

In brief, there is nothing that authority and the official world dislikes as much as something which has no precedent, and the *Amsterdam* was unprecedented to a degree which put her outside the scope of Britain's museums or Government departments. She was no one's responsibility as an historic monument.

Having ascertained how far she was complete, our next step was to decide a plan of campaign: what the aims of the investigation were to be and what the ship's real significance was. Many were ready to give advice, most of it conflicting. Some urged that we should simply excavate the ship's contents, saying that it was unnecessary to record the form and construction of the vessel herself, since there was a full contemporary record of Dutch East Indiamen. The *Amsterdam*, they said, was not after all so very old. As compared with the thousand years old Viking ships preserved at Oslo, she had only two and a quarter centuries behind her, and being so comparatively recent she could offer us little. There was no real need to spend days, weeks even, making a detailed study of her form and construction.

I could not share this view. Contemporary documentary records are a poor substitute for the modern scientific study of an actual ship and its contents, and I was determined that we should not pursue this policy. Nevertheless, there is a vast store of contemporary VOC documents – 1 kilometre of shelving in the State Archives at The Hague are filled with them – and one is bound to encounter the argument that eighteenth-century wrecks are too modern for detailed archaeological study.

The answer is simple and straightforward. It is just because of the great wealth of record that we do need archaeological studies. The historian will always welcome additional written records on any subject of any period, because of the added depth they give, and the richer understanding of the complex forces that shape man's destiny. In the same way the modern scientific study of an exceptionally well-preserved historic shipwreck, such as the *Amsterdam*, allows us to arrive at a far more detailed knowledge and understanding of life, technology, trade and other aspects of the past than the written record alone will allow. Anything less than a properly researched and detailed study would be a denial of our responsibility to those who come after us, as well as to archaeologists, historians and the interested public today. Truth is not always as obvious as it may seem, and the false and misleading conclusion from a misunderstanding of the archaeological and documentary evidence is fatally easy. We must handle even eighteenth-century sites with the same care that we would give to those of an earlier period. They must not be dismissed as irrelevant, for it is in this case the very rare combination of a well-preserved wreck and the rich contemporary record which adds a new dimension to the study and fuller understanding of the past upon which our modern world and societies are founded.

Nor would I rest the claim for the full excavation and preservation of the *Amsterdam* on her value to history and archaeology alone. She is of value as an educational project, for she is one of the finest creations of human technological skill of her time, and her preservation will give everyone the chance to walk the decks of a type of ship that made one of the great maritime empires of history.

Not, of course, that there was not a temptation for some people to rush back to salvage the wreck site, which obviously held so many more antiquities within her nearly intact hull, lying just where she was wrecked on that wild Sunday afternoon in January 1749. It would be so easy to continue salvage with the aid of the mechanical excavator, and to disregard the fact that this method would mean irreparable damage to a great proportion of the antiquities inside her, and almost more important, the loss of the information to be gained from seeing them in their natural context. If we were to do this, the effect would be rather like driving a bulldozer through a house. There would be a pile of rubble and, mingled with it, broken crockery, ornaments, furniture, clothing, and all that had formed a vital part of the life going on inside its walls. How much better it would be to embark on a careful excavation, and find each object in the place where it was used.

As far as I was concerned, the *Amsterdam* should be excavated properly or not at all. Each deck should be explored in turn, with a record made not only of each item found, but of its exact position in the ship before it was disturbed. Then, when the ship had been fully excavated, she could if necessary be restored exactly as she was – the house would be fully and exactly furnished. Nevertheless, a little digging and disturbance had first to be done, if we were to obtain the essential information.

Thus our present investigation would be a survey of the ship to ascertain with an absolute minimum of excavation:

1. How much of the ship had survived.

2. How much of her contents of cargo, stores and personal possessions of passengers and crew remained.

These could only be undertaken during the special tidal conditions, but there were two further aims of a related kind, apart from the actual excavation:

3. Discovery of the documented history of the ship.

4. Compilation of a scientific record of all antiquities found in 1969, which would be related to the small group of earlier finds already in Hastings Museum.

Having sketched out the campaign, I once more consulted the Admiralty tide tables, and confirmed that in the last week of September 1969 the *Amsterdam* was once more due to appear, and I would be able to have my first sight of her.

9

The First Excavation 1969–70

Seeing the wreck for the first time, under the great arc of a sunny sky on that level shore, I was initially struck by its remoteness. Here was the focus of those weeks of discussion, the seemingly endless careful planning, a slightly projecting, elongated outline, which suddenly seemed as elusive to tackle as those shellfish on the beaches of childhood which dig themselves into the sand away from small groping fingers. The warmth of the day meant that many holidaymakers were about, and our equipment rapidly attracted them to the site, unmistakable with its brilliant orange marker buoys, each attached to a steel post. These posts marked off the four corners of our working area, and were linked by a rope to keep it clear of curious sightseers.

We went to work immediately the first low tide made a start possible, and set up our basic survey line running down the middle of the wreck from bow to stern. Bill Wilkes had marked the line in alternate half metres of black and white, and as we set about measuring the sides of the ship in their relation to it, the *Amsterdam* emerged as a vessel of substance, and more so when the members of the team had scoured her aged timbers free from mussel shells and seaweed. With her bluff rounded bow pointing towards the land, and her almost flat stern confronting the sea, she was frozen in that moment when on 26 January 1749 she ran ashore. In pounding against her port side the high seas had apparently eroded a scour pit, partly undermining the hull and causing her to lean over at 18° to port. It was at this angle that she had sunk into the beach, and I calculated that the deck beams on the port side were those of the upper gun deck, and, on the starboard, those of the lower gun deck.

From the outset it was clear that the measuring of the ship alone would take a long time, and to give us a good start we decided to work a night shift. After an evening meal and a pleasant discussion in the bar of the Warrior

Hotel in Hastings, I returned to my lodgings to prepare my record of what had already been measured that day. This, too, took a long time, and left me with only an hour or two's sleep before rising again to catch the next low tide at three in the morning!

Walking along the sea front in the middle of the night seemed strange. Quite deserted, it was very dark, very quiet, and very close to the time barrier. The rhythmic splash of the waves on the sand was a sound which went back beyond the era of the *Amsterdam* to when there was no human history at all. Only occasional cars speeding anonymously along the coast road gave an insistent reminder of the present. We all met, as arranged, at the site office of William Press & Son Ltd., just inland from the wreck, where we changed and made our way down the beach.

The sun of the previous day had left the inheritance of a mist which swirled round us, cutting off by its dank curtain all trace of sleeping Bexhill and Hastings, and isolating us in a weird world of our own. The yellow glow of the floodlights spilled over the wreck area, and we moved like ghostly shadows following our task of measuring. Apart from the sound of the generator, we had lost the twentieth century, the beach was eerie and the light sound of the sea in the still blackness outside our working area gave a renewed sense of time standing still. Here in the very domain of the sea, where the tide would run above the level of our heads in a few short hours, the shade of Willem Klump, anxiously pacing the sands once again seemed very close; and the hollow echoes of the shouts of the Dutch sailors carrying the treasure chests up the beach were almost audible. Archaeologists deal with facts, and are not supposed to be carried away on journeys into the past, but on that night those events of a long-gone age seemed disturbingly near.

As our measuring progressed and the results were recorded on paper, the *Amsterdam* herself also began to come alive in the most amazing fashion. We were re-creating her two-dimensionally, and at the end of seven days Bill Wilkes and his wife, Ann, were as exhausted as myself. The builders of that complex masterpiece of a ship never dreamt of the labour they would one day put us to. Bill was my main aid in the measuring, and Ann was always there, quietly ready to help at every stage, whether it was holding the other end of a tape measure, or writing down notes from our dictation, or guarding our precious stock of photographic equipment, or simply explaining to yet another inquirer what all the fuss was about. Ann and Bill stand equally high on the list of people who made a very substantial contribution to the success of the investigation. Hard though we worked, however, by the end of the week of especially low tides, it was clear that we should have to leave

1. An aerial view (above) of the *Amsterdam* site showing the outcrop of clay and remains of the prehistoric forest of *c*. 3000 BC into which the ship sank; and (below) a metal detector survey at sunrise which revealed details of objects lying within the ship on the deeply buried lower gun deck.

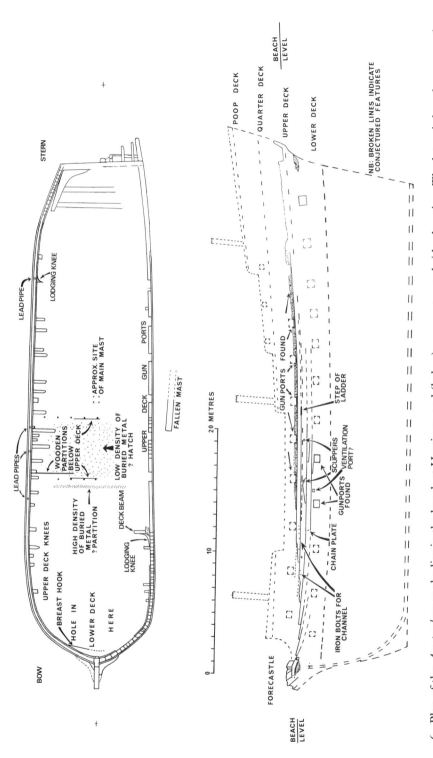

BOW

LEADPIPE

LEAD PIPES

STERN

LODGING KNEE

UPPER DECK KNEES

BREAST HOOK

HOLE IN

LOWER DECK

HERE

HIGH DENSITY
OF BURIED
METAL
? PARTITION

LODGING
KNEE

DECK BEAM

WOODEN
PARTITIONS
BELOW
UPPER DECK

'APPROX. SITE
OF MAIN MAST

LOW DENSITY OF
BURIED METAL ? HATCH

UPPER DECK GUN PORTS

FALLEN MAST

0   10   20 METRES

FORECASTLE

IRON BOLTS FOR
CHANNEL

CHAIN PLATE

GUNPORTS
FOUND

SCUPPERS

VENTILATION
PORT?

STEP OF
LADDER

GUN PORTS FOUND

POOP DECK

QUARTER DECK

UPPER DECK

LOWER DECK

BEACH
LEVEL

NB: BROKEN LINES INDICATE
CONJECTURED FEATURES

BEACH
LEVEL

6. Plan of the *Amsterdam* as she lies in the beach at Hastings, and (below) a reconstructed side elevation. The latter is based on our 1969 survey excavation and probings into the seabed in and beside the wreck, and also upon a careful study of contemporary models and records of Dutch East Indiamen. The stern has been revised to include the preliminary results of the excavation in 1984 by Jon Adams and Jerzy Gawronski of the Amsterdam Foundation.

XII. Overall view of the *Amsterdam* excavation site in 1969, with the upright supports of the partitions standing clear of the sand towards the centre of the wreck.

completion of the job until the sea once more retreated, in January 1970.

Before the end of our first stint of detailed measuring in the September of 1969, it was clear that a good deal of the interpretation of the visible upper deck features would depend on what we could discover of the lower gun deck. Since, however, we did not intend to uncover any of this, there had to be an alternative means of obtaining the information, and I decided to excavate a hole outside the ship, so that we could record at least one gunport of the lower gun deck. The best position for this would be forward of the fallen mast, because although the mast was so deeply buried below the beach that it would not be affected by the machine driving across its line, any excavation close to its side might disturb its fastenings.

Almost at the last moment, however, William Press & Son decided to dissociate themselves from further commitment to work on the *Amsterdam*. It was a major setback, since there were no funds to hire them; and it was only because the BBC had already made special arrangements to film the excavation that we were able to proceed. Rather than cancel their filming and stop our investigation, they hired the men and such necessary equipment as an excavator, a pump, and floodlights to carry out the work. Neither they nor we were to be disappointed by the result.

Yet it should not be thought that the decision to excavate the two holes alongside the ship had been made lightly. The risks involved had been very carefully weighed against the potential gains. We were less fortunate than those who had worked on the 17th century Swedish warship, *Wasa*, for she had stood clear of the sea bottom in the still waters of Stockholm harbour and her hull could easily be examined to see whether the timbers were securely fastened to each other, or whether they would need pegging together before work could be begun. The sea would not allow us the leisure to strengthen the hull, and in any case we had to excavate first to find out whether it would be necessary. The fact that the *Amsterdam* had already withstood one series of excavations at the hands of William Press suggested that the timbers would hold. If they did not, the probable extent of damage had to be estimated, and it seemed, in view of the size and careful placing of our points of excavation, that if it did occur it would be minimal. Without the resulting information we would have to make our plea for total excavation and, if possible, preservation merely on the strength of some very interesting ideas about that roughly oval outline of ship's timbers in the seabed. Ideas alone would not stand up against critical archaeological review, let alone against the practical objections of the people in whose hands the organisation of the enormous funds needed to put such a scheme into operation would be. The

XIII. A close-up of the model of the *Mercurius* (above) showing the deadeyes, with the supporting wooden shelf or 'channel' below them, and chain-plate links below that, while above them can be seen how the rope lanyards were threaded through them, and they were joined to the rigging. A gunport similar to those on the model is seen below being carefully measured by one of the divers in September 1969 when an exploratory excavation revealed part of the port side exterior between the upper and lower gun decks.

Amsterdam would continue to lie there, unprotected by any law with 'teeth', increasingly at the mercy of the sea as the years passed, and pillaged by human enemies. If practical steps were to be taken to bring about her recovery, then we must act now.

The first of the crucial low tides occurred on a Friday evening, starting about sunset, and once again the historic ship was to experience a mechanical excavator at work, but this time as a friend and not as a destroyer. The shovel rapidly dug down into the sand immediately outside the vessel just forward of the middle of the ship on the port side to find a lower deck gunport, and soon the characteristically square shape of the upper part of a gunport, closed by a port lid, came clearly into view about 1.5 metres down. As the brilliance of the floodlights fell upon it, this was a most exciting moment for me. Having seen with my own eyes evidence of the completeness of the ship, I was determined to do all that was humanly possible to get her raised.

Just as I had instructed the operator of the excavator to dig to a depth of 2 metres to uncover the lower part of the port, a scarf joint in the planking above the gunport sprang about 10 centimetres from the ribs, and all the water in the scoured interior of the ship seemed to erupt from the hole. Quickly, the sandy sides of the hole we had dug slumped inwards, making it wider and shallower, so that by the time the contents stabilised the excavator could no longer reach its arm far enough forward to the side of the ship to continue digging at the precise point we wanted.

This cut down our working time, but quickly and efficiently the pump operators drained the water from the hole. The lower gunport we had first found now having been rendered inaccessible, I asked for the excavator to be moved forward so that the hole alongside the ship could be enlarged sufficiently for the next one to be laid bare, for it was essential that we secure a record of at least one of them. The steel teeth of the excavator bucket bit rapidly into the sand again, and once again the top of a gunport appeared. Once we reached 1.5 metres, however, in an effort to go deeper, the sand was like water and flowed in from the sides of our hole to keep the bottom of the gunport submerged.

We should have to go ahead with recording it just as it was, except for some cleaning up. Bill Wilkes was landed with this dirty work, for although it wasn't altogether incompatible with measuring, it certainly couldn't be combined with the notetaking and photography which I must do. Even before we started digging this last hole, it had become plain that there would be no time on site to make the scale drawing of the elevation of the ship's side which I had hoped. I decided to rely upon sketches, measurements and

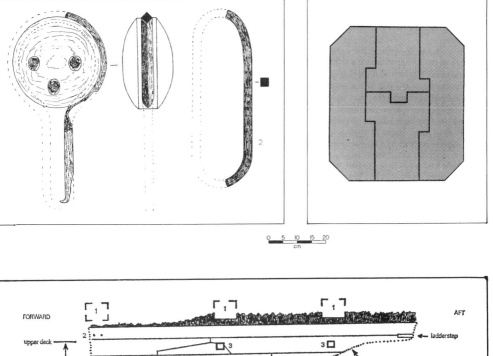

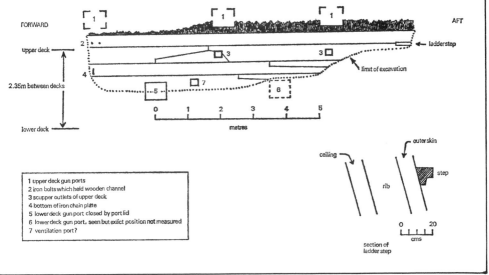

FORWARD

AFT

← ladderstep

upper deck

2 : .

3

3

limit of excavation

2.35m between decks

4 :

7

5

6

lower deck

0   1   2   3   4   5

metres

1 upper deck gun ports
2 iron bolts which held wooden channel
3 scupper outlets of upper deck
4 bottom of iron chain plate
5 lower deck gun port closed by port lid
6 lower deck gun port, seen but exact position not measured
7 ventilation port?

outer skin

ceiling

step

rib

0   20

cms

section of
ladder step

0   5   10   15   20
cm

. Five wooden deadeyes were found (above left) apparently still attached to the port side of the
ship, opposite the location of the foremast. Each of them (1) was bound with a wrought iron link of a
chain plate. The rope lanyard passing through the three holes of the deadeye was 3 cm in diameter.
Part of another chain-plate link (2) was also found. The cross-section of the mast (above right),
probably the mainmast, which had fallen on the west side of the ship, and of which a considerable
length still lies in the sands, was drawn by John Manwaring Baines. The exterior elevation of the
port side of the ship (below) as exposed in the archaeological excavation of 1969, shows the upper
deck gunports (1), the iron bolts which once held the wooden shelf or 'channel' (2); upper deck
scupper outlets (3), the lower end of a chain plate (4); closed lower deck gun ports (5) and (6); and
what may have been a lower deck ventilation port (7). One step of the ladder up the ship's side was
also found (section inset).

photographs, all of which would be related to a vertical datum line that would be set up for the purpose. As quickly as we could we measured the dimensions of all the plans and other construction details, and supplemented my overall sketch with a series of photographs in both colour and black-and-white.

The construction detail was in itself of considerable interest. The planks varied in width between 35 and 47 centimetres, and were about 10 centimetres thick. The gunport top lay at a depth of about 1.4 metres, was 65 centimetres wide and about 50 high, and was closed by a port lid on which I could clearly see the corroded iron bolts which had once helped to hold it to the ship's side. In overall size, it differed little from the ports by the upper gun deck.

The scupper outlets, each some 20 centimetres square, were now clearly seen, and one of them gave us constant trouble by continuing steadfastly to do the job for which it had been made in 1748. Water from it poured straight onto Bill, working immediately below, and efforts to block it failed in a way that was a tribute to its design. In the end the problem was solved by placing a polythene bag full of sand on the inward side, and allowing the water flow to suck this into the scupper where it became firmly wedged and still remains.

Forward of the gunport, and at about upper deck level, the elevation now showed part of a horizontal row of iron bolts, each 4 or 5 centimetres square. This find was important because the bolts once held the wooden shelf or 'channel' projecting beyond the side of the ship. Ninety centimetres below this was an iron bar of the chain plates which once held the thick flattened balls of timber, pierced to hold the rigging for the foremast, which are known as deadeyes. When the 'channel' had been destroyed the deadeyes had fallen alongside the ship. The William Press excavation had destroyed the links of these chains, but each of the seven deadeyes handed into Hastings Museum had traces of corroded iron at their edges, showing that these were the lower deadeyes, and not those of the upper rigging which would be held by rope. One fortunately had enough chain plate still attached for its almost complete reconstruction to be achieved, except that the beginning of the rounding of the lower end of the chain link may be due to its being bent by the force of the mechanical excavator, rather than an indication of the normal size of these links.

Taking a break from cleaning while I took measurements at the forward end of the hole, Bill Wilkes had his reward. He found a cache of broken Dutch clay pipes from Gouda in the sand beside the ship at the after end of the hole. These must have been part of the cargo, since they were not only all unsmoked, but also some still had their bowls filled with buckwheat packing. They had probably been broken when thrown overboard in the course of the salvage attempts of 1749, for the depth at which they were found showed that they were filling the scour hole which had been formed at the time of the wreck on the port side of the ship. The sand in which they were imbedded was also in contrast with the clay deposit which otherwise surrounded the ship as she sank into the shore.

Our final record was to be of the ship's 'tumble-home', this curiously expressive term refers to the special shaping of the hull needed to ensure that such a large and heavily armed ship as the *Amsterdam* did not capsize through being top heavy. The effect was to make her sides slope inward so that the higher decks above the water line were narrower than those below to just the right extent to bring the great weight of her cannons closer to the centre line and ensure her stability. Bill devised a simple and effective instrument to enable us to measure this degree of slope very accurately. It consisted of two long pieces of angle iron, bolted together at a right angle, and with a spirit level affixed to one. When the latter was horizontal, we knew that the former was vertical. For good measure, the vertical side was graduated in alternating black and white 10 centimetre sections so that the instrument also served as a scale. Using this, we took offset measurements, and established the precise angle of slope of the upper part of the port side of the ship.

Measuring, drawing and photographing, the two of us had had no time to glance seawards, and it took a hail from someone outside the excavation to warn us that the tide was visibly creeping across the beach and was already nearly lapping the stern. Taking a few last notes, I moved the recording equipment out of the hole, and left Bill, kitted up in his dry suit, to finish the collection of hundreds of fragments of broken clay pipes lying in the sand almost beside the ship's ladder. Minutes later the sea edged over the rim of the scoured hollow in and around the ship, and within a very few minutes thousands of gallons of seawater were pouring into the wreck. Successful, but dripping wet, Bill climbed out of the hole with the last of the pipes he had collected. Meanwhile, the pump had been disconnected, the lights were soon doused, and our equipment hoisted onto lorries ready to be driven up the beach to safety.

Early next morning, in a dull grey dawn with a trace of drizzle carried on a chilly wind, we moved all our gear back again. This time we planned to dig a hole on the opposite side of the wreck, near the bow, which would give us a different profile. For a depth of three metres the excavator immediately brought up mud, instead of the scour-hole sand of the previous day. It was a grey clay, sticky to the touch, and we were obviously now cutting through the original geological formation.

As before, Bill did the dirty work of cleaning up, while I tried to keep my hands unsoiled and dry for notemaking and the taking of photographs: the notebooks bear witness of some failure here. Our second hole did not fully live up to our expectations, in that we found the whole side of the ship to be covered here with a deposit of 'iron pan', a concretion caused by the deposition of corroded iron in solution from sources elsewhere in the wreck. As a result, we could do little more than take another profile of the hull and examine the upper part of the ship's side.

That morning tide was a short one of barely an hour, so that when Bill and I had completed the examination just described, and had taken our hull profile, it was time to move out as the sea washed in once more. As it did so, one more secret of the *Amsterdam* was revealed, for as the water filled the interior of the wreck again, the added weight began forcing the planking from the hull timbers. The hole outside the ship, though filling rapidly with water, was not doing so quickly enough to arrest an outward movement of the planking, but none of the ship fell apart as a result, and we at least knew for certain that corrosion of all the iron fastenings must be very considerable. The planks and ribs would need bolting together again during the final excavation.

One major problem remained. Though we now knew that two-thirds of the ship had survived, the condition of the lower gun deck and the under part of the hull remained uncertain. If the enormous financial backing needed for complete excavation, raising, and restoration of the ship was to be found, we had to persuade our sponsors that not only had the hull survived complete to within a metre of the ship's gunwale in her waist, but that a substantial part of the contents within that area also remained.

Digging inside the ship before the final excavations could not be contemplated, but there might be another way of 'looking' at what was not normally seen. The *Amsterdam* would surface again in January to March 1970, the period of the longest and lowest tides of the year. I explained my idea to Rod Garfield, of Hymac Ltd, a leading manufacturer of excavation equipment, and, with the approval of his directors, he set about organizing what was needed. First he found a pump manufacturer, Itt Flygt Ltd., prepared to drain 70,000 gallons of water from the scoured hollow round the ship, and to do it free of charge. Next, Hymac themselves provided two mobile high-level platforms, one 30 ft (9.14 m) high, and the other 50 ft

(15.24 m) for taking photographs.

In January we would concentrate on continuing measurement of the ship's construction and on making trial runs with the platforms, in the hope that conditions would be suitable for photograhy. Both clear visibility and a calm sea would be needed, for a gale could nullify to a great extent the degree of tidal 'pull' producing the really low tides we hoped for. What we got was rain and a storm somewhere out in the Atlantic which bottled up the water in the English Channel so that the sea level above the *Amsterdam* stopped falling far too soon. Nevertheless, Bill Wilkes and several others waded about waist deep in the bitterly cold sea to continue the measuring of essential features.

Fortunately, I had planned the pumping operation for March, and our luck then changed. We were even grateful for those January storms which had scoured a quite deep hollow ready for us and, as the tide fell, it became clear that once the ship was pumped out we would see parts of the vessel not visible since 1749. The Flygt pumps took about half an hour to drain the 70,000 gallons of water inside the *Amsterdam* back into the sea. It was impressive.

Walking down into the hull the moment it was clear, I could see the underside of the upper deck, where it survived on the port side, and also its supporting knees. And, even more important, I could plainly see the tops of three transverse wooden partitions, which had separated off the cabins. Of the two main ones, the first crossed the ship just forward of the main hatch, and the second just aft of it, except where the William Press excavators had torn it away in the western or port half of the vessel.

The *Amsterdam* was offering knotty problems the more we considered her. The most obvious was that presented by her having heeled to the west, so that the port side is deeper into the beach than the starboard, and yet the posts of the partitions stood vertically. This indicated that the lower gun deck may have partly collapsed down into the hold on the starboard side, for the posts did not link up with the angle of the visible deck beams on both sides of the ship: to port they went up at an angle into the air, and to starboard they went down at an angle into the sand, and the two angles did not meet. Although it was most likely that the deck beams belonged to both upper and lower gun decks, and that part of the latter had collapsed into the hold, it was obviously essential that this question should be resolved as soon as possible, since it would materially affect our understanding and interpretation of the entire structure.

I decided to use a thin pointed steel rod to probe the beach and find an

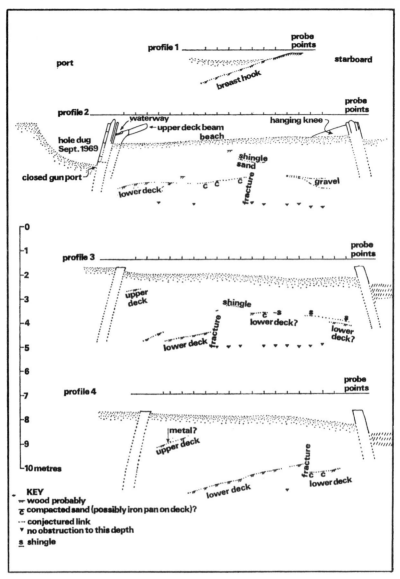

8. Probed profiles across the *Amsterdam*: (1) along the breast hook, which should accurately show the angle of the ship at the bow; (2) shows how the upper deck knees, on opposite sides of the ship, are not correctly aligned (indicating a squeezing together of the sides of the vessel which photographs confirm); (3) indicating the unevenness of the lower gun deck, and its possible fracture owing to its partial collapse onto the hold; (4) taken from the stern shows the lower gun deck largely complete, though perhaps fractured. The inclination of the deck, being the same as the breast hook in the bow, probably shows the correct inclination of the entire wreck (see also proton magnetometer survey in fig. 9 and position of probed profiles p. 97).

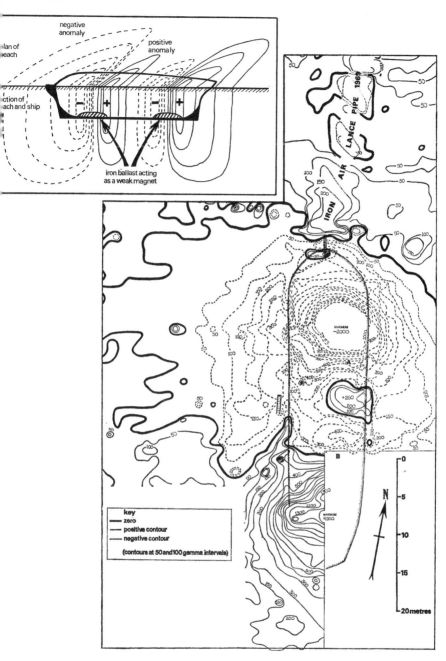

9. A proton magnetometer survey carried out by Jeremy Green showed variations in the Earth's magnetic field caused by two great masses of iron ballast (at a depth of 8–9 metres) in the bottom of the ship at A and B (see also diagrammatic sketch inset). Since these are east of the vessel's centre line, they confirm that the ship has heeled over to the west (to port) in its entirety.

answer. This decision was not made without misgiving, for although this new test could not damage the ship's structure, it could damage small objects, especially of glass or pottery, which might come in its path. Yet if we were going to ask others to expend great sums on excavating and raising the ship, then there was a duty to find out exactly what we were asking them to raise, and the possible damage to a few objects would be a small price to pay for such information.

The probe was carried out during our last survey of the ship during the low tides of August 1970, and, having set up five horizontal lines across the ship, we probed along each of these at intervals of 50 centimetres to obtain a series of cross-profiles. The first profile was along the breast hook in the bow, and this showed a very steep angle of tilt. Approximately midway between the upper and lower gun decks, the breast hook only just emerged from the sand on the starboard side, and I found no trace of any supports for the upper deck, so that this deck must have rested on the breast hook which had recently been *in situ*, but had since been placed in the garden of Hastings Museum by the William Press men.

The second profile ran between partitions and showed that the lower deck on the west side ran away at an angle from the side of the ship, although just a little distance in (about 1.5 metres from the side) it curved downward to become horizontal. Close to the ship's middle the probe struck what felt like hard compacted sand, which I could well imagine might have formed on the lower deck, and when we moved to the starboard half we found the probe went through a variety of layers of shingle, which must have simply accumulated in the ship. Strangely, there was no indication of the presence of the lower deck, which lay only 2.7 metres below the upper, and it seems likely that there is a longitudinal break in the lower deck from stem to stern, as is also suggested by the other profiles. The deck would appear to have collapsed downward in the starboard half of the ship. We also recorded gaps in the lower deck which were evidently caused by missing planks.

The third profile, taken nearer the stern, showed a similar lower deck structure, but here the deck has apparently collapsed in the middle of the vessel on the assumed line of fracture. The fourth and final crosswise profile, taken in the stern, showed that the port side of the hull seemed to be standing about 1.8 metres above a fairly broad portion of the upper gun deck. Here the two decks are 2.3 metres apart, and the lower is complete from one side of the ship to the other, though the longitudinal fracture still seems to be present. The lower deck slope at the stern is similar to that of the breast hook at the bow, and as both are attached to the ends of the ship, they presumably show the true angle of tilt of the *Amsterdam*. In the middle of the ship there has clearly been much distortion, especially to starboard, and indeed this shows in photographs taken looking along that side, for the hull actually curves inwards slightly, presumably as a result of external pressure. The fifth profile taken longitudinally across the stern established the curving shape of the 'counter' between the two gun decks, and was probed several times.

Among the interesting finds in and around the ship made by William Press's men, especially on the west side, had been many traces of rigging, including pieces of iron-stained rope as well as one of the loose wooden rope ends. Their most important above-deck discovery, however, was a considerable length of the fallen mainmast. As already mentioned, it snapped in the maw of one of their excavators, but the quick thinking of John Manwaring Baines ensured that the event was at least photographed, and it was he who later unravelled the complex construction of the mast in a drawn cross-section.

In the eighteenth century there were no trees of sufficient size available to shipbuilders to make large masts of one timber, so that they were normally made from a series of interlocking timbers bound together with rope. One of the William Press men mentioned that he thought he had seen traces of the rope binding, but it was very fragile and had been destroyed during the following high tide.

In this way we managed to achieve the aim of finding out how far the *Amsterdam* was intact and the main lines of her construction, with a minimum of excavation. We had established that she was two-thirds complete and had gained some idea of the conservation problems she would present, as well as such difficulties as fractures, distortions, and corroded iron fastenings which will confront those who raise her. Nevertheless, it all added up to a ship incomparably worth protecting, raising and preserving. To achieve that would involve a change in the British law, and an enormous public relations effort in Holland.

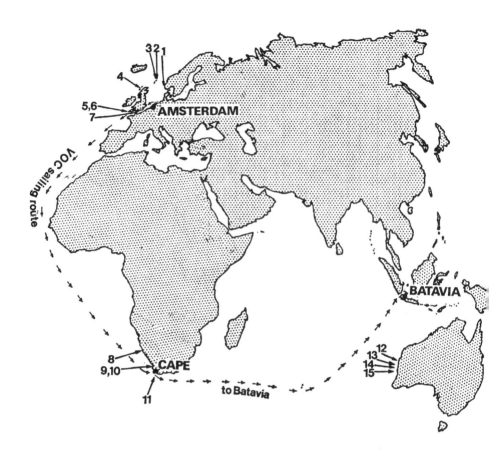

10. The East India Company sailing route from Amsterdam to Batavia, via the Cape, giving the names of the earlier wreck sites of Company ships to be discovered. The concentration on the coast of Western Australia, where excellent work has been done, was due to the vessels either losing their way or being blown off course.

1. *Akerendam* 1725	8. Unidentified wreck in Meob Bay c.1746
2. *Lastdrager* 1653	9. *Merestijn* 1702
Kennemerland 1661	10. *Middelburg* 1781
3. *de Liefde* 1711	11. *'t Huijs t'Kraijensteijn* 1698
4. *Adelaar* 1728	12. *Zuydorp* 1712
5. *Hollandia* 1743	13. *Batavia* 1629
6. *Princesse Maria* 1685	14. *Zeewyk* 1727
7. *Amsterdam* 1749	15. *Vergulde Draeck* 1656

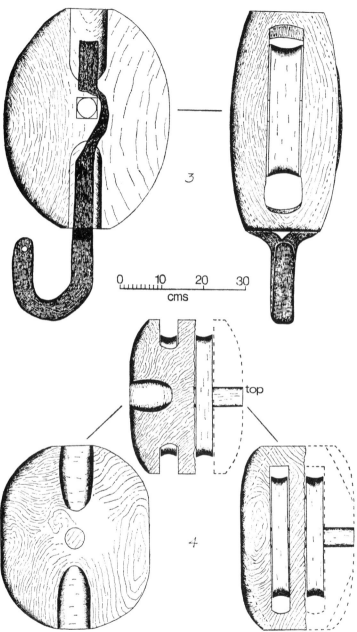

0   10   20   30
cms

11. **Pulley blocks 1**. These come from the ship's store on the orlop deck in the bow. The block with the iron hook may have been used in loading and unloading cargo and equipment.

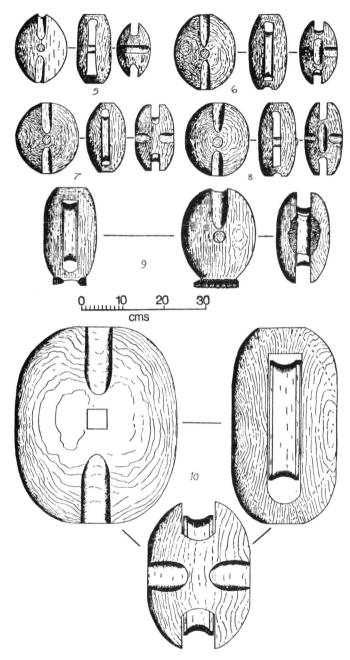

12. **Pulley blocks 2.** A variety of other types, used in rigging the ship, from the same store; the centre one (9) is part of a fiddle block, in which two blocks of differing size were attached end to end, so resembling a violin.

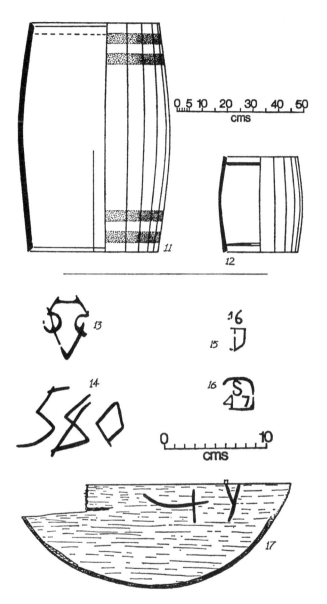

13. **Barrels.** A reconstruction of one of the barrels. These were used not only for beer and water (one had traces of an internal coating of pitch to make it waterproof), but as general purpose containers. Traces of corrosion on the staves showed the placing of the iron bands. The small keg of tallow (12) had been branded (15 and 16), and a much larger barrel about 1.20 metres high, had a stave branded with the Company mark (13). A barrel 192.8 cm high had the number 580 carved on one stave (14) and a section from a barrel end (17) carried part of an inscription.

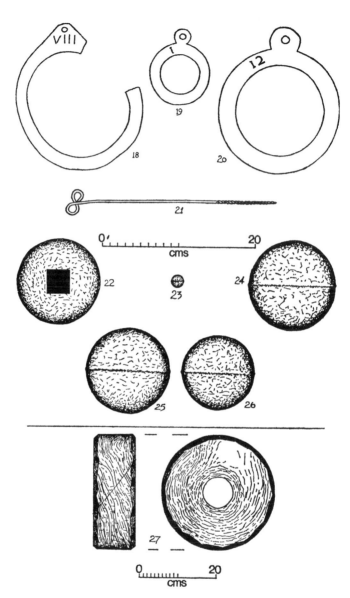

14. **Armament 1.** Bronze gauges to check the size of the ship's 1 lb, 8 lb and 12 lb cannon balls (18–20), to prevent a mis-cast ball jamming the weapon and causing an explosion; and one of several bronze reamers (21) for piercing and cleaning the cannon touch-hole. Half a bar shot (22): in these an iron bar linked two balls, and they were used to bring down the enemy rigging. The two largest cannon balls here, 11.5 cm and 11 cm diameter (24 and 25), were for use in the 12 lb cannon, and the smaller, 9.5 cm diameter (26), was for the 8 lb cannon on the upper gun deck. At the bottom (27) is a wooden gun carriage wheel.

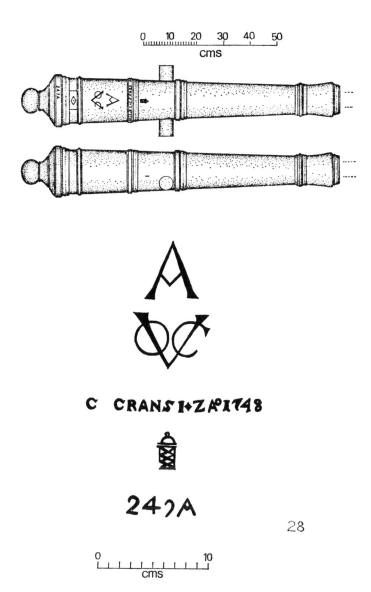

28

15. **Armament 2.** Five identical guns of this type (28) were found on the lower gun deck, each with a 55 mm bore and firing a 1 lb ball. Each gun was inscribed with the VOC insignia and a crude representation of the arms of the city of Amsterdam, three crosses below a crown. They also carried the gundfounder's inscription, showing their maker was Cyprianus Crans, of Amsterdam. This gunfounder supplied not only the VOC but clients as far afield as Portugal.

16. **Glass.** Several square green glass bottles (29 and 30) of different sizes were broken by the mechanical excavator in 1969: one still contained a cork, so that they may have held wine or gin. At least sixty green glass wine bottles of squat (31) or slender (32) shape were recovered intact from the lower gun deck. Jack Aaron, chief diver on the sewer outfall project, graphically described how the gas in each bottle sent them bobbing up to the surface. Many corks, some 'waisted' with use and others new, were washed away, apart from a handful saved by John Manwaring Baines. The majority of the bottles were of the squat Dutch type and when one was submitted to Mr A. C. Simpson of the testing and quality control laboratory of Internation Distillers and Vinters at Harlow in Essex, it was found to contain red wine 21.7 per cent proof, which showed that it had been fortified, probably with brandy, to help preserve it. The tall, more modern design contained wine which was only 14.5 per cent proof, which may have been some of the new Bergeraque wine known to have been aboard. Degeneration over time and contamination by sea water gave the wines an indescribable smell and a very strong and unpleasant tang. Neither was analytically identifiable with any individual present day wine, but there was a considerable similarity to some modern wines. One complete specimen of the simplest type of wine glass used with them aboard the *Amsterdam* was found long ago (35), and finds in 1969 included fragments of four other types (33, 34, 36, 37). There were also parts of four clear glass cups, one with a simple cut decoration (38), two with an engraved or scratched design (39 and 40), and the fourth with an engraved design of rather different form (42). A small clear glass panel (41) of unknown purpose has a scratched decoration resembling that of cups 39 and 40, and there were many small fragments of greenish window glass (not illustrated), about 2 mm thick.

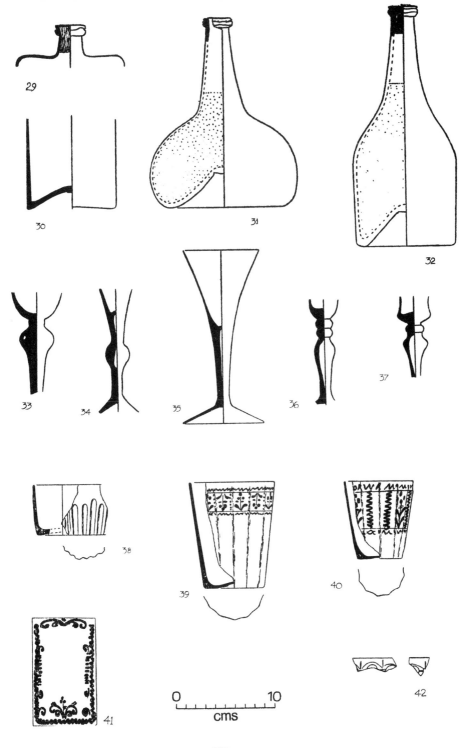

29

30

31

32

33

34

35

36

37

38

39

40

41

0   10
cms

42

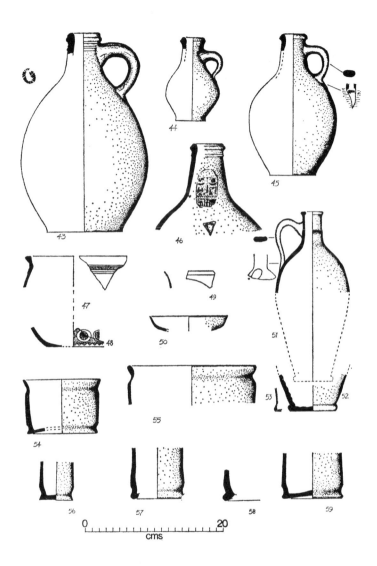

0 ━━━━━━━━━━━━━ 20
cms

17. **Pottery 1.** The hard-fired stoneware jugs found on the lower deck may have contained gin. They included mottled brown stoneware undecorated except for occasional stamps, as shown beside the first example (43) here, though one has a very crude 'Bellarmine' mask (46), and in one the cork was in position, but only seawater was inside. Of pale grey stoneware pots one type, a jug with a neck band in cobalt blue (51), had varying base forms (53, 53), the other had an incised decoration (48); both types were made in the Low Countries. There are also fragments of a pale grey saltglaze stoneware cup and saucer (49 and 50). Delftware drug jars from the surgeon's stores (54–59) are in a yellow or buff-coloured ware with a white glaze.

128

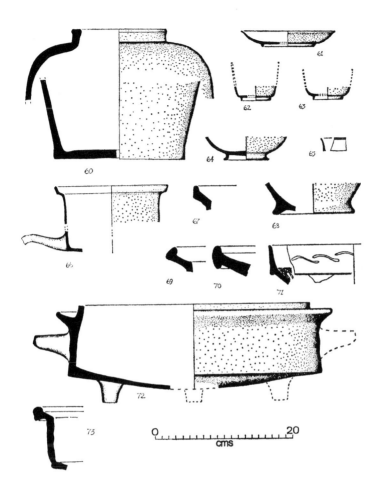

18. **Pottery 2.** The Asian storage jar (60) is of pink ware with a matt chocolate-brown surface slip. At least four saucers of white Chinese porcelain have been recovered (61), each with blue floral decoration and a brown colour between the rim and foot ring, as well as small fragments of cups with a matching blue decoration: these are likely to have been personal possessions of the officers or passengers, rather than standard Company issue. The fragments of small bowls (64 and 65) with a dark brown glaze over a red-brown body may be English Astbury ware. An interesting find was the pot with the handles and probably three short legs, made of buff coarse ware, with a green glaze inside and on the rim (66). A fragment of light brown coarse ware (68) is the base of a brown glazed bowl or jar, and the remaining pottery fragments all formed part of large grown glazed dishes, of which some probably had three short legs (72), and one (71) has an applied white clay decoration in addition to its brown glaze. These were probably intended for use in cooking.

19. **Miscellaneous finds 1.** A leather knife sheath (96), decorated with tulips and inscribed at the top 'ANNO 1744'; another knife sheath (97), very worn through use, but originally decorated with a lattice design of which traces still remain; a wooden handle with two holes at each end for iron nails, probably to attach it to a door (98); a small portion of a wooden pot (99), of which the missing base would have fitted into the groove near the bottom which is partly shown in the section; a fragmentary wooden object with a series of holes (100), of which the purpose is uncertain; two wooden pegs, both broken at their lower end (101 and 102); a circular wooden ramrod for use on the guns, still containing some rope, and pierced at the waist by an iron nail with which it was secured to the rope (103); the end segment of a hardwood flute with an ivory terminal (104), the maker's name being stamped on the wood 'B (?) HEMSING'; a large sheet of lead of unknown purpose (105), decorated with two geometric patterns which each have a pair of holes with a small brass fitting between them, showing that some object once fitted into position there, and inscribed VH, possibly the owner's initials – it has been damaged and distorted in the course of its excavation; and three cast-iron weights (106–8), stamped on top with the date 1748, their value (two for 3 lb and one for 5 lb), and the ligatured letters IR (perhaps the mark of the weights and measures inspector). The last-named were recovered from the lower gun deck, where they were perhaps used with a substantial pair of scales (not yet found) to weigh out food and other supplies from the ship's stores.

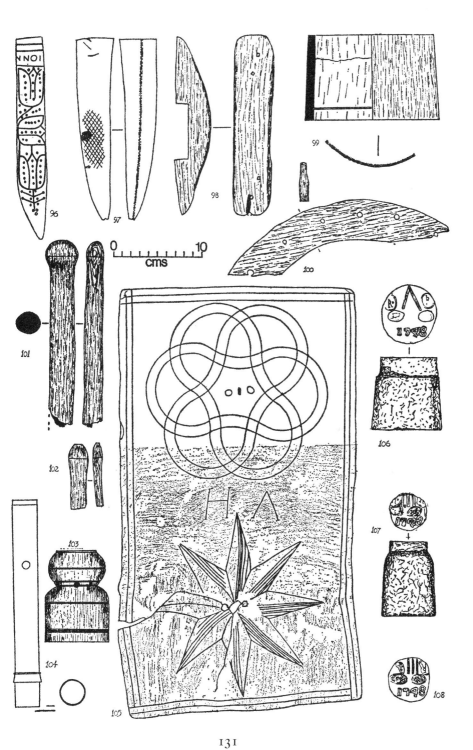

20. **Miscellaneous finds 2.** These included a bronze pot lid (109); a bronze cauldron (110), tinned inside and originally having three small legs and a handle; a bronze pot, perhaps a kettle (111), with a broken handle, which was so crushed when found as to make this reconstruction uncertain, and a bronze lantern hinge (112), to which the candle-holder (117) probably belonged. Particularly fine was a group of nine almost identical bronze candlesticks (113), some of them coated with tin on the outside to simulate silver. The upper part screwed into a base, the latter having makers' marks stamped on the footring (two are unclear, but five have winged angels, and two a tree). From their number and the buckwheat husks preserved in the concretion on those which had not been cleaned, these seem to have been part of the cargo; an alternative form of candlestick base was that into which a candle holder was screwed (114), this example having lost both holder and the bottom of the base. One of three bronze smoothing irons (115) found on the lower gun deck had lost its iron base plate through corrosion, and like its companions had a broken handle, but the lidded compartment still contained remains of the once red-hot charcoal which had heated it. This shows that it was in use aboard, perhaps to iron the officers' uniforms. The pewter tankard with a hinged lid (116) has part of an Amsterdam maker's mark below the rim which includes the arms of the city. There were also four fine-toothed ivory combs (118), and a single horn comb distorted in drying (119); two wooden needle dollies with screw-on lids (120 and 121); pewter and bronze buckles – a curved pewter one, possibly for a shoe (122), part of a flat bronze buckle, maybe for a belt (123), another curved pewter buckle (124), two curved bronze buckles (125 and 126), part of a bronze buckle (127), and two flat bronze buckles (128 and 129). Of four sticks of red sealing wax (130–3), one has the maker's mark KOK beneath a crown and two have burnt ends – possibly having been used by Klump himself. Of the buttons 134–8, all are bone except 135, which is pewter.

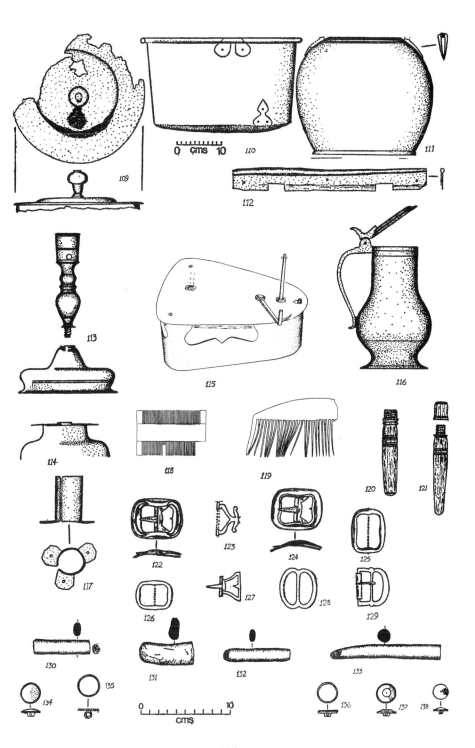

109

110

0 cms 10

111

112

113

115

116

114

118

119

120

121

117

122

123

124

125

126

127

128

129

130

131

132

133

134

135

136

137

138

0 cms 10

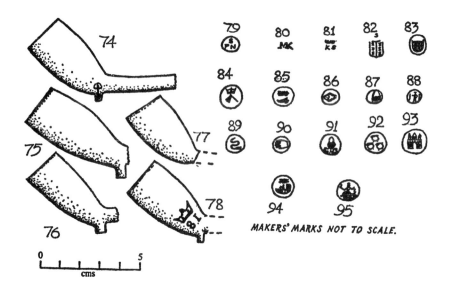

MAKERS' MARKS NOT TO SCALE.

21. Clay pipes made in Gouda were found in and beside the *Amsterdam*, their range in shape and size being indicated here. The makers' marks were identified by Adrian Oswald on the basis of S. Laansma's manuscript list of Gouda manufacturers of the period 1724–1865; goddess of fortune (74), Ary Vertuijen; crowned 81 (78), Cornelis van Zon; PNS (79), probably Pieter and Nanne Schenk (used only in 1746); MK (80), Jan Korthalz; KS (81) Jan Lorijn; arms of Gouda, with an 's' above indicating that it was one of the standard run (82), (the mark was used only after 1739); parrot's cage (83), Benjamin Weeldenburg (died 1746); an axe crowned (84), Jan de Vrind; shoe crowned (85), Ary Mulaart or Salomon Lamor or Jan Oosterhout; fish (86), Gerrit Verschuit; writing hand (87), Hage van Kinse (used only in 1746); King David? (88), if so then made by Jan Girbo; snake (89), Cornelis van der Wal or Lucas de Jong; right hand (90), Dirk Reijswijk; acorn (91), unidentified maker; three pots (92), Leendert van der Ring; probably three turrets (93), Jan de Vrind; child in a cradle (94), Cornelis Gruiztershof; Bacchus on a vat (95), Anthony Kalf. Other pipemakers represented by examples in the *Amsterdam* are Anthony Dilbaer or Matejs van der Ring, Jacob van der Kist, Willem Schippers, Jacob Goedoet, Klaas Verbij, Jan van Leeuwe, Tennis Veregge, Jan Puyt, Willem van der Valk.

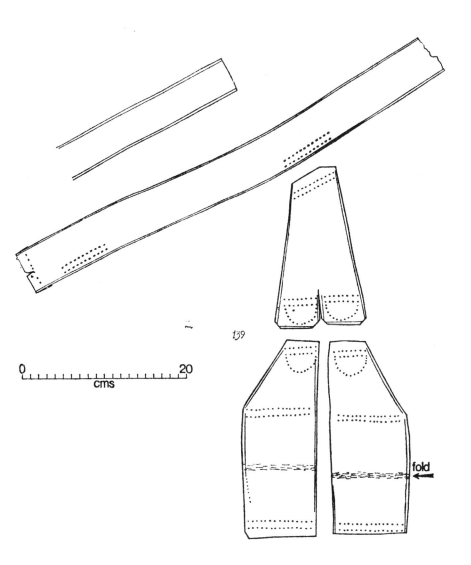

0 |—————————————| 20
cms

139

22. **Sword belt.** Fragments of a leather sword belt have a lattice pattern on them (not illustrated) which marks them as Company property. The individual pieces were sewn together in the order shown on the drawing. The sword scabbard lay in the folded lower part of the leather attachment hanging from the belt, and stitch holes at the end of the belt itself indicate that there was a buckle and a second hanging attachment there to secure the scabbard.

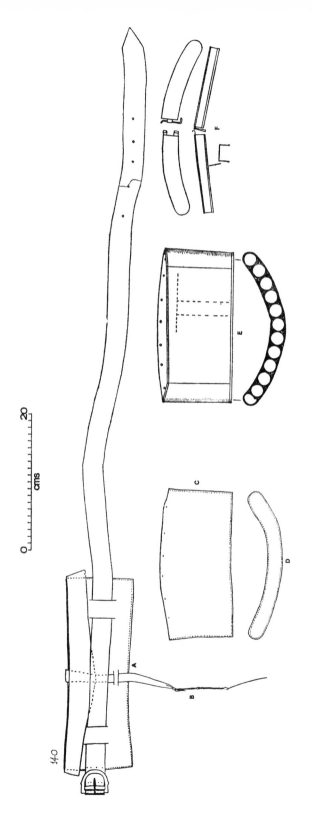

140

23. **Cartridge belt.** One of at least thirteen military cartridge case belts found, which all had the same Company lattice pattern on them as the sword belt, and a bronze buckle. Each also has a leather pouch (ACD) to hold a lidded bronze case (E) with 12 cartridge chambers, the cartridges being protected by a double-hinged lid (F). From the pouch hangs a special small leather and bronze pricker (B) to clear the touchhole of the musket. Not even a small part of a musket has yet been found, but many small lead musket balls have been recovered, some stored in a wooden barrel.

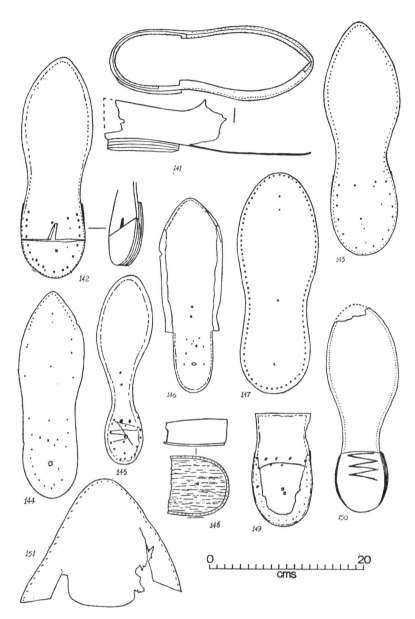

24. **Shoes.** Only parts of shoes were found in 1969, since they were torn apart during the excavation. Most were men's, and where the undersole survives, there are clear traces of wear, but one (145) is particularly interesting as it is part of a woman's high-heeled shoe, and presumably belonged to one of the ship's three lady passengers. Most of the heels are leather, but one (148) is wooden, with a leather surround. In one case part of the leather upper survives by itself (151).

25. **Cutlery**. Only the handles probably of knives have been found (152–7), the blades having long ago corroded away, and these were all of wood, except for two of ivory or horn (154 and 155). All had the lower end of the handle held by a bronze ring. Several of the pewter spoons (158–68) are of special interest. The one with a design of a Dutch 'hooker' scratched in a bowl (159) has the stamped initials IA, possibly those of Jan Aalders, one of the young seamen, and the worn pewterer's mark on the handle shows that it was made in Rotterdam; the broken spoon (161) bears the initials of its young merchant owner, AB – Andries van Bockom – and the pewterer's mark shows that it was made by Hendrik van Duyreland of Rotterdam; the broken end of a spoon handle (162) has the owner's initial W scratched on it twice; the intials PBS on the next one (163) mark it as having belonged to Pieternella Bockom Schook, the wife of Andries van Bockom; the one with a number of circles drawn with a compass in the bowl (164) conveys an incomplete attempt at decoration; next comes a specimen (165) with the mark of the Amsterdam pewterer Barend Geel; and the last three have owners we can tentatively identify – the initials IB suggest that two (166 and 167) belonged to Jurriaan Bartels, one of the two 'Second Mates' or Onder Stuurmen, in the ship, and the scratched initials CI almost certainly show that the last one (168) belonged to Christoffel Jasper, one of the gun-captains or Busschieters. The melted end of one of the spoons (167) and the marks of intense heat on one of the others are interesting because, since the *Amsterdam* never caught fire, the damage may have occurred when an attempt was made in 1749 to burn through the deck to try and salvage the cargo. For the fate of these spoons, see page 145.

152 153 154 155 156 157

159

enlargment of bowl

158

160

161

162

163

164

165 166 167 168

0 ⌊⌊⌊⌊⌊⌊⌊⌊⌊⌊⌊⌊⌊⌊⌊⌊⌊⌊⌊⌊ 20
cms

10

Ensuring the Future of the Amsterdam

Within two days of beginning work on the *Amsterdam* in 1969 we knew that she was unique. The extent of her preservation was somewhat comparable with that of the 17th century warship *Wasa*, which had been raised from the depths of Stockholm harbour in 1961 for display in a special museum in that city, but the *Amsterdam* represented a 'time capsule' of 18th century life which combined both military and civilian aspects, including as it did even women aboard. Certain that she must be preserved, we had to choose. Should we take over ownership of the ship and keep the bulk of the items on board in Britain, or should we offer the *Amsterdam* back to the Dutch people? As salvors in possession of the wreck, we were not required to make any approach to the Dutch Government, since English law gave us substantial rights. Hastings Council also took independent advice, and found that they, too, had rights in the matter.

Nevertheless, as a professional archaeologist and historian, it seemed to me, as it did to my colleagues, that the Dutch nation had the prior right and that we should consult them as to whether they wished to take home the ship which was such an intimate part of their great past. The cost would be large, and our resources were small as compared with those which the city of Amsterdam and the Dutch Government could muster to complete the work as it should be done. We decided to offer them all the help we could if they were interested, and, if they were not, we would seek to establish the facilities to excavate the ship ourselves, and consider preserving her at Hastings.

The first priority, however, was to ensure that the wreck survived long enough to be preserved. The results achieved by William Press with a

XIV. The lower deck supports of the starboard side being recorded (above) during the archaeological survey of 1969, and (below) a view from above of the excavation of the port side.

mechanical excavator had been given great publicity, so that it would obviously be only a matter of time before other 'treasure hunters' followed suit, and even souvenir hunters armed only with a penknife could whittle away dangerously at the upper part of the wooden structure when it showed above the sands at the seasonal low tides.

For the British Government the *Amsterdam*, as a wreck in our territorial waters, could be either a hazard to shipping, in which case she should be destroyed as soon as possible, or potentially salvageable. Since she obviously didn't come in the first category, she must come in the second, and procedure was governed by the Merchant Shipping Act of 1894, which had no clauses dealing with wrecks of historic or cultural importance. It was under this act that William Press, as 'salvor', had already carried out their obligation to deliver to the Receiver of Wreck the articles they had recovered. Under his other 'hat' this official was the local Customs Officer, who gave us all the help on the spot that the law would allow, but in matters of urgency, or for policy decisions, we had to approach the administrators of the Marine Division of the Department of Trade in High Holborn, London.

Curiously, the 1894 act did not protect shipwrecks on the seabed, even though diving was by then sufficiently advanced to have made such a provision sensible. Once any articles were brought ashore, however, they had to be handed over to the Receiver, and if, in his opinion, they were worth more than £20, they had to be itemised, together with any identification marks, and the list displayed at Lloyds in London so that anyone with a claim to ownership might recognize his property. This is not so absurd as it might seem in the case of an ancient wreck, for in the case of another East Indiaman, the *Hollandia*, wrecked off the Scillies in 1743, Baron Bentinck of Gorssel, descendant of one of the women passengers, had declared his interest in a copper-gilt shoe buckle and the silver cutlery bearing his family arms.

In such cases the Receiver acts as 'umpire' between the salvor and the owner, to ensure that a suitable salvage award is paid. On the other hand, if there are no claims, the items are sold, the salvor receiving a large part of the proceeds and the rest going to the Crown. These provisions, reasonable enough for ordinary commercial wrecks, were an invitation to legal plunder in the case of historic ones. Nor was this the only danger. Objects aboard a historic wreck may have reached a point at which deterioration is either very slow or almost completely suspended. Raise them to the surface and the results are often swift and sometimes disastrous. Iron may oxidise so rapidly that it becomes too hot for the safety of the salvage boat, and the object may have to be thrown overboard again, and bottles of wine have been known to explode under the change of pressure when they are raised from the sea bed.

Once ashore, and in the store of the Receiver of Wreck, further deterioration is likely. Nothing could have looked more solid and sturdy than the *Amsterdam*'s wooden pulley blocks, as they were raised from the water. Yet, as they dried, some of them split open pitiably. Iron continues to oxidise in air and items from the ship were soon lying in pools of liquid oxide. Bronze items were less affected, but a few started 'growing' the greenish surface bloom which marks the onset of 'bronze disease', especially where iron and bronze were stored close to each other, for iron oxide is an initiator of bronze disease. Even the corks in the wine bottles shrank, once exposed to air, and not only made the contents evaporate, but allowed the entry of bacteria to contaminate the wine.

It was the more trying to an archaeologist that such things happened even more often now than in the early years when officialdom had been inclined to dismiss everything not obviously as of intrinsic value, such as gold, silver and jewellery, as 'old junk'. The Department of Trade had awoken to the possible value of all antiquities, and wanted to establish the original ownership of every object, so that it could be disposed of in the correct legal way – if any of it survived the period of storage.

In the case of the *Amsterdam* the antiquities in the care of the Receiver of Wreck had no legal owner, and should have remained untouched, but Hastings Museum, the Fishbourne Roman Palace Museum near Chichester, and the Guildhall Museum in the City of London, all undertook some conservation work. They did so, despite the meagreness of their resources, and with the knowledge that their work would enhance the value of the objects so making it more difficult for museums to buy them. However, at least the objects would survive. In the meantime, while we worked towards changing government policy, we felt that, despite the increased risk of the wreck being plundered, publicity should be encouraged, in order to make our aims for this and other wrecks better known.

Angela Croome, then secretary of the Council of Nautical Archaeology, arranged for the journalists to visit the site on 10 March 1970 (the date of the lowest tide) and held a press conference afterwards in Hastings Museum. Luckily a debate in Parliament coincided with the excellent press coverage, and the *Amsterdam* was included in the discussion of the fate of historic wrecks. It was decided that the possibility of giving legal protection to historic wrecks should be reveiwed by a government committee.

This was excellent, but immediate protection was what we needed.

Having failed with the Marine Division of the Department of Trade, helpful though they would have liked to be, we turned to the Ancient Monuments section of the Department of the Environment. But, not even for Nelson's *Victory* could the regulations be stretched to allow a ship to be covered as an historic monument: the *Amsterdam*, like other ships, had been designed to move, and was therefore classed simply as a chattel! Overwhelmed by the very thought of responsibility for such a thing, the Department achieved the further safeguard of deciding that the limit of their jurisdiction for anything at all was the high water mark. We were referred back to the Department of Trade.

Actually, what we wanted partly lay so close at hand we had failed to recognize it. Hastings Council had the power to pass its own bye-laws, and if it could stop people playing football among its rosebeds, it could surely take the *Amsterdam* under its care. Consequently, when an anticipated attempt was made to plunder the wreck, our 'warning system' allowed us to be informed immediately and we instantly took steps to stop further damage.

When, in 1973, the Protection of Wrecks Act became law, the *Amsterdam* was one of the first four historic wrecks to be designated. It was a start, but the 'protection' still did not rule out commercial activities by those lawfully engaged in wreck exploitation, and archaeologists and museums had still to live with their saleroom consequences. The number of protected wrecks was also limited to about two dozen. This was understandable administratively, but with approximately twenty thousand square miles of British territorial waters to be covered, it was monstrously inadequate. Sweden alone has 400 of her historic wrecks under government protection, and even this is a minute fraction of the 20,000 known.

Besides protecting the antiquities still in the *Amsterdam*, we were most anxious to see that those already raised should find a proper home where further conservation could be carried out, preferably in a Dutch museum. George Naish, then Keeper of the National Maritime Museum at Greenwich and a member of the Council for Nautical Archaeology, was speedily in touch with Gerrit van der Heide, at that time director of the excavation of the historic wrecks endangered by the Zuyder Zee reclamation scheme, and also with Humphrey Hazelhoff Roelfzema, director of the Scheepvaart (Maritime) Museum in Amsterdam.

Both came to Hastings early in our investigations, the former as a Dutch Government observer, and we were glad to establish this particular link, since we hoped that the Dutch Government would put in their claim for the finds before they had to be disposed of by the Receiver for the British Crown.

Initially, rather to our alarm, the Dutch Government regarded the *Amsterdam* as a commercial salvage proposition, on the model of other VOC wrecks where the only remains were items left on the sea bottom, the ship itself having disintegrated. Their Ministry of Finance duly made a claim for the salvaged items, but, for some of them, the claim unfortunately came too late. Two of the bronze guns (see colour plate 2) were found to have disappeared from the security store of William Press at Eastbourne, and the pewter spoons of Andries van Bockom, his wife Pieternella, as well as the spoon with the ship engraved in the bowl, had been stolen from Hastings Museum. These, too, had been photographed, and subsequently a few parts of the spoons were recovered by the police, but these did not include the ship engraving, or the spoon owned by Pieternella. Also, the guns remained lost, and it is sad that, perhaps as ornaments in a Sussex garden, they can no longer take their place in the story of the ship.

However, our immediate fears for the wreck itself were soon put to rest when the Ministry of Culture became involved, and in 1971 a special Anglo-Dutch technical commission was set up to report on the possibility of excavating, raising and returning the ship to Amsterdam for preservation and display. The Dutch Government indicated that the cost would be too high for them to undertake the work, and it was obvious that what was needed was an independent organisation to do so under government aegis. In March 1972, dining with Vernon Leonard on a visit to Amsterdam, I discussed with him the need to make the Dutch people better acquainted with their lost possession on the English coast. (Until then most of the press coverage had been in Britain.) As editor of the colourful monthly news magazine *Holland Herald*, Vernon Leonard could run a story that would help to save the ship, especially as the city of Amsterdam was to celebrate the 700th anniversary of its foundation in 1975. What could be more appropriate than to make the scheme for raising the ship the focal point of the celebrations?

An opening £1000 was donated by *Holland Herald* itself, and four thousand copies of a specially commissioned picture of the *Amsterdam* at sea by Jan Poortman were sold. Groups of readers, from the students of Weymouth South High School in Massachusetts, who held an exhibition, to the customers of the Old Ship public house at Styal, near Manchester, who held a raffle, made their contributions, and many individuals sent along a cheque if only 'just to save a splinter' as one donor wrote. Commercial firms also helped, and Jan Mastenbroek, chief publicity officer of the City of Amsterdam, was quick to support the project. A party of Dutch officials visited Hastings in August 1972 to see the wreck site and the finds in the museum for themselves, and also to watch a showing of the BBC *Chronicle* film. They decided to establish a non-profitmaking foundation to administer the project, and a special report, largely funded by the £5000 raised by *Holland Herald*, was to be prepared. Thenceforward, all our endeavours regarding the *Amsterdam* were in support of this scheme.

II

The Excavation of 1984

Once the Foundation for the VOC ship *Amsterdam* had been established in Holland in 1975, representing as it did, not only the ministries of Culture and Finance, but the City of Amsterdam itself, real plans could be made. The reports of committees which covered each of the chief aspects of the project – excavation, raising, preservation, display, and fund raising – showed that the estimated overall cost of three-and-a-half million pounds was justified. It was also clear that the *Amsterdam* would fill the gap between the early 19th century HMS *Victory*, and the 17th century warship *Wasa*.

Since the depth of water over the ship was only nine metres, the proposed method of eventual recovery was by enclosing the entire area of the wreck within an outer circular dyke and a small inner cofferdam, so that the site could be pumped dry for the excavation of the ship and the preparation for her return to Holland. In March 1975 boreholes and probes confirmed that, although the ship was lying in a thick bed of clay, its bottom was resting, at a depth of eight or nine metres, on a bed of sandstone. The sheet piling of the steel cofferdam would have to be sufficiently deep to 'grip' on this, or the walls of the dam might collapse inward.

Next, in August 1978, wood samples were taken from the wreck so that various methods of conservation could be tested in advance. Mechanical excavators again returned to the site, this time digging holes next to the stern on the port side, and nearly amidships on the starboard. Apart from being completely waterlogged, the wood was found to be scarcely different from modern timber, and an international conference in Amsterdam under the auspices of UNESCO in 1979 decided that the best way to preserve the hull would be to allow it to dry out gradually under controlled humidity. Fortunately, this was also the cheapest method.

147

Full funds for the recovery could obviously not be raised at the outset, so it was decided to mount preliminary excavations by divers, especially since the interest of further finds would undoubtedly speed the flow of contributions. The successful recovery of the *Mary Rose* along these lines had been encouraging, but ours was much the bigger task. Instead of the one third of the Tudor ship that had survived, we had two-thirds of the hull intact, lying on an open shore, and several days' voyage from her eventual home along the Channel and across part of the North Sea. In addition, the *Amsterdam* was closely packed with cargo and supplies for a voyage to the other side of the world, and the objects within the vessel were extremely concentrated. These initial excavations would also enable the eventual major effort to be planned with greater precision, showing more exactly what would be needed in the way of staffing, accommodation, and conservation facilities, and – not least – giving us much badly needed information about the physical condition of the ship and its contents.

The chairman of the board of the Amsterdam Foundation, Mr dr Charles van Rooy, announced that a committee had been formed to organize an excavation in 1984, with Olaf Heyligers at its head. The latter had already made such contributions to Anglo-Dutch understanding that he had been awarded a CBE, and though he had retired from public life he tackled the task with great enthusiasm.

Funds of £100,000 were allocated for the 1984 season, and a combined Dutch and British team of divers was assembled, while I, having been intimately involved in the planning of the ship's recovery, was invited to act as director. It was an invitation I could not decline, especially as the excavation, being on British territory, needed someone who was familiar with the legal aspects of British archaeological sites.

Since this was apparently the first major archaeological excavation anywhere to be carried out underwater in the inter-tidal surf zone, the method had to be carefully considered. It was proposed by Franz Lous, the Foundation's technical engineer, that a working platform should be constructed adjacent to the *Amsterdam*, since a boat moored there would undoubtedly be damaged by constantly hitting the seabed at low tide during the three months on site, and might itself be wrecked in a sudden gale before it could be towed to a safe haven. This platform was constructed during the extreme low tides of March-April 1984, and was to work extremely well.

Sheet piling was also driven into the sand round the stern half of the ship, the top only rising half a metre above the seabed, since it was intended only to retain the clay round the ship as the excavation deepened, and thus take

XV. A diver coming in at high water to the working platform used in the excavation of 1984 (above), and (below) the shaped timber base of the officers' toilet, with the opening through which the waste pipe passed seen left. Jon Adams is measuring it in the water tank to prevent it drying out too quickly and losing shape.

XVI. A few of the many bottles of red wine (above) found in the ship in 1969, and (below) some of the bottles as they were found, packed in straw in a wooden chest, on the sea bed in 1984.

VII. A drinking glass found in 1984 (above), just large enough to hold a dram of spirits, and just the same as is used in the Netherland today; and (below) stoneware jugs, which may have held gin, found on the lower gun deck in 1969.

pressure off the hull. The piling also served to support four long steel girders which spanned the ship's stern, and held survey points for the archaeological recording of the site. We also used a computer lent to us to operate a program devised by Nicholas Rule for the *Mary Rose* excavation, which converted diagonal measurements downward from the survey points into horizontal eastings and northings, and depth.

Each section of the project team had its own supervisors, Jerzy Gawronski and Jon Adams were in charge of the team of volunteer divers, twelve to fifteen in number at any one time, drawn both from the Netherlands and Britain. Jerzy was especially interested in the archaeology of the Dutch East India Company, having been involved in the partial excavation carried out on the *Vliegend Hart* (Flying Hart), wrecked off the Dutch coast in 1735, and having also studied (as I had myself) many of the items recovered from the *Hollandia*, which sank off the Scillies in 1743. Jon Adams was a professional North Sea diver, and as senior diving archaeologist on the *Mary Rose* had, among other things, been responsible for inserting the cables into the hull prior to its successful lifting in 1982. More recently he had directed the underwater excavation of the *Sea Venture*, sunk in 1609 off Bermuda, for the Sea Venture Trust. The boat carrying divers and equipment between platform and shore was piloted by Peter Barrie, a local man with a good eye for wind and weather.

Wendy Robinson, backed by Dr Ton Jütte and Peter Vos of the Central Laboratory in Amsterdam, undertook the temporary conservation of the objects, whose registration was in the care of Chris Vastenhoud. These activities and the photography and administration were all carried on in the excavation headquarters in the former ballroom of a nearby holiday camp. Our beach compound consisted of a Portacabin lent by the Hastings Tourism Department and two large storage containers sent over from Holland, one for storing diving gear and the other for equipment to maintain a generator and air compressor, serviced by an engineer kindly provided by the same firm, Smit Tak, which supplied the equipment. He soon had a metal pipeline laid across the seabed to take compressed air out to the platform to operate the airlifts. These plastic hosepipes, about ten centimetres in diameter, are vital tools for underwater excavation. As compressed air is pumped into the lower end, it bubbles upwards inside the pipe to create the effect of a vacuum cleaner. Both the surface demand diving equipment and our underwater video was on loan from Comex, a company which carries out underwater work in the North Sea oil industry. The complex task of administration on limited funds was eased for Gerrit van der

XVIII. Part of the surgeon's equipment. To the left (above) the large syringe he would use in administering an enema; and (below) the wooden nozzle which would be attached to introduce the enema into the rectum. Behind it are two of the drug jars from his stores.

Heide by much local help from Hastings.

At the end of June the work began. The uppermost sands and silts in and around the stern, as expected, contained almost no artefacts. For years they had been repeatedly washed away and redeposited by the tides and currents. Beneath them were the more interesting deposits of silt, sand and gravel which had been disturbed by mechanical excavators digging inside the stern in 1969 and yet again in 1971. Here broken objects of glass, pottery and metal were scattered throughout the layers, but since they were not in their original location, it was unnecessary to record their exact position.

Gradually the hull structure was revealed, with part of the upper gun deck on the port side, and part of the lower gun deck on the starboard. The deck levels had a 20° list to port, and bore the marks of earlier treasure-hunting activities – the 'teeth marks' of the mechanical excavators, and parts of smashed objects, especially wine bottles and pottery jugs. If ever justification were needed for the 1973 Protection of Wrecks Act, then the damage to the *Amsterdam* caused in 1969 and 1971 would be sufficient.

Damage to the interior of the stern had been expected, however, and it was heartening to discover as the excavation was enlarged that the hull itself had remained largely intact. Indeed, I was delighted to see that more of the ship had survived than I had previously thought, for, above the counter on the port side, there were three of the nearly vertical timbers that once formed the framework of the stern gallery to the upper gundeck. On the other hand, it was disturbing to find that, as a result of the excavation of the consolidated filling in and around the ship in 1969 and 1971, the structure of the hull, though still largely complete, was showing signs of breaking up. The original iron fastenings holding the timber together had largely corroded away, leaving only the silts and concretions to support some of the timbers.

Even though the timbers had remained buried, some had become detached and others had evidently been washed away during the few years before we carried out our excavation. Some timbers that we recovered were especially interesting in that they included three loose planks from the counter at the stern, which contained a small ventilation window to the lower gun deck, and which also revealed that the inside of the hull had been painted grey-blue.

As the excavation proceeded through July and August an increasing amount of the lower gun deck appeared within the vessel, and on the outside the top of the sternpost was located, giving us our first glimpse of the rudder position. I was interested to find, in confirmation of the contemporary letter to John Collier in 1749, that the rudder was missing, having been lost in the

XIX. The leather cover of a book (above), with a very wide spine, seen to the left, which may have been a Bible. Recovered in 1984, it was photographed while still wet, and the tooling can be seen far more plainly than today, when the leather has dried. Below is a collection of clay pipes from the cargo, recovered in 1969.

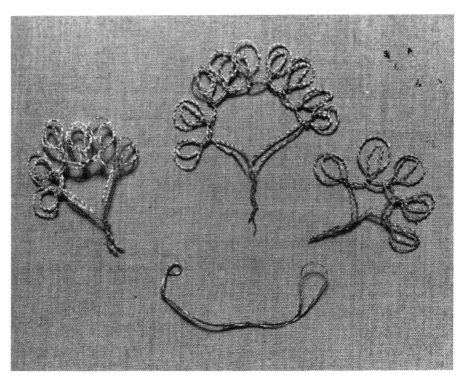

XX. Samples of ornamental 'frogging' (above), possibly from a man's costume, recovered in 1984 and (below) the 'twin' cufflinks, one recovered in 1969 and one in 1984, which most probably belonged to someone serving in the ship.

26. A typical mid–18th century lady's dress, with a reconstruction of the quilted silk 'petticoat', decorated with a heart and flowers design, of which a fragment was found in the *Amsterdam* in 1984. It was evidently a dress of quality, and most likely belonged to Pieternella or Catharina Schook.

27. **Miscellaneous finds 3.** In 1984 many items of the ship's equipment and personal possessions of those aboard were found. A plank (top left), branded with the East India Company insignia; the incribed lead casing of a barrel (centre left), perhaps once containing butter, seems to read 'No 8, GIANT', followed by a three-leaved clover, or perhaps a shamrock, since it is known that cheap Irish butter was on board for consumption by the crew; and (bottom left) is the cover of a thick book, perhaps a Bible. Of the dress accessories found (top to bottom right), the finest was a small artificial flower of silk on a bronze wire frame; others included a silk bow, probably from a man's hat, a cheap necklace of dark glass beads on bronze wire, a seal on top of a corked wine bottle (maybe a merchant's mark), and many beautifully decorated buttons, made (as is the one illustrated here) of bronze on a wooden base. All these objects were drawn by Pru Theobalds for the Amsterdam Foundation (various scales).

storm while the ship was still out in Pevensey Bay. What really first brought the dig alive for me, however, was the discovery nearby of the lid of a wooden chest carved with Captain Willem Klump's initials. It probably came from one of the five chests of wine and spirits listed in the paybook in his name, and had presumably fallen from a stern window of his cabin on the quarter deck after the ship had run ashore.

In excavating round the ship's stern on the port side, several more important features were revealed, notably the semi-circular wooden shelf or base of the quarter gallery which had once supported the toilets for the officers. Although all of the superstructure of the gallery had been lost, a hole in the shelf, which had originally taken the waste pipe from the toilets, revealed its former use. The timber was not quite in its original position, having slipped and been 'concreted' onto the side of the ship again at an angle. When cleaned it was found to have been roughly inscribed A–VOC. More exciting, however, was the discovery below the quarter galley of part of the ship's decoratively carved wooden stern. I had hardly dared hope that any of this survived, and was delighted to find that even the fragment we found – a looped fish tail – was for Bas Kist and Herman Ketting of the Rijksmuseum (both VOC specialists) enough to suggest what had been the design of the entire carving (see p. 161).

However, the richest recoveries were, as one would expect, being made inside the ship. Drug jars and parts of three syringes could almost certainly be assigned to the stores of Hendrik Brumleij, the ship's surgeon, and a tally stick was probably once part of the equipment of Floris de Vos, the Constapel (Master Gunner) whose living quarters lay in the stern. The bones of the hind quarters of pigs could equally certainly be assigned to the cook's stores of salt pork: we were constantly turning up staves of broken barrels that presumably once contained the pork. More romantic, and surprising in the state of its preservation, was part of a woman's long quilted dress, in silk with a heart and flowers design, which probably belonged to one of the sisters aboard. Perhaps once associated with it was an exquisite artificial flower made of silk supported on bronze wire.

As the excavation came towards its end in August, the divers at last reached the levels which had remained undisturbed since 1749. It was a strangely moving moment. Here there was a thick layer of silt about two metres wide and a metre thick, which could be traced for five metres from the stern along the port side of the lower gun deck. The first impression was one of confusion, no doubt partly caused by this having been the lowest part of the sloping gundeck, so that objects had slid and rolled to accumulate here in

1749. However, on closer study it gradually appeared that the objects fell into related groups: gun appurtenances and other equipment for the VOC soldiery; food in wooden barrels, and bottles of wine still in their straw packing inside their wooden chest; and clothing, particularly shoes and a boot, and other miscellaneous personal items such as gaming marbles and dice, and the cover of a book.

Thousands of objects were recovered in this summer of 1984, which will take years of research and more background excavation to establish their full historical significance. Even some of the very many small brass pins, often found in wrecks, were unusual in that they still had clear evidence of their packaging arrangement, something I have never before seen. Part of the cargo, perhaps privately owned, since it was not in the ship's hold, included fragments of 'precious' red Mediterranean coral, which was presumably being exported to the Far East for use in inlay work.

We had only just begun to examine our finds when the end of August, and the end of the favourable tides and weather, brought the excavation to a close, though with the certainty of further important discoveries in the future. During September polythene sheeting was taken under water, with some difficulty, and laid over the unexcavated deposits. Two of three lead-clad barrels that had been located were left in situ, and there was time only partly to empty the wooden chest containing the wine bottles. Finally, with sandbags in position, the excavation was deeply backfilled with sand and silt to protect it from the winter gales.

Of the three absolutely complete lead-clad wooden barrels found in the ship, one was raised and provisional analysis showed that it contained only animal fat, perhaps butter. The legal complications, which prevented our immediately sending this fragile and unstable object to the Central Laboratory in Amsterdam for much-needed and urgent conservation, became something of a *cause célèbre*.

Although the excavation finished at the end of August, it was not until 20th November that most of the recovered objects were at last legally released from Britain and were returned to Amsterdam, whence they had started out on their never completed voyage 235 years earlier. At least, however, they avoided the irreparable damage they would have sustained three days later when an exceptionally violent storm devastated the holiday camp in which our archaeological headquarters lay.

The legal difficulties were substantial and would have had a funny side, if the objects themselves had not been caught up in excessive delays in reaching the conservation laboratory. The amount of form-filling required, and the

XXI. The beautifully carved 'fishtail' decoration which ornamented the ship exterior at the base of the quarter gallery containing the officers' toilets on the port side. Poor visibility meant that Jon Adams had to photograph this 1984 discovery a section at a time to produce this composite picture; inset to the right is his drawing of the complete feature.

sometimes contradictory clauses of the forms themselves, would have made life difficult if we had been dealing with a small, steady flow of objects from a land site. But, we were racing against the clock on an underwater site, trying to beat the deterioration in large quantities of items rendered most unstable by being brought to the surface, and get them as quickly as possible into the safe hands of the Central Research Laboratory in Amsterdam.

From the point of view of the Receiver of Wreck the vital question was ownership: the owners of property recovered from a wreck must have the opportunity of reclaiming it, and the items listed on the appropriate forms must be divided into two groups. One comprised objects such as the lead-clad barrel, which could with reason be assumed to be the property of the Dutch Government in succession to the extinct VOC, and must be claimed on their behalf by the Ministry of Finance. This was duly done. The other, and smaller, group of objects comprised those which were obviously personal possessions, such as the wooden box lid bearing Willem Klump's initials. These would have to wait a year for claimants to come forward, and if none did, they would become the property of the British Crown. The Amsterdam Foundation could then acquire them from the Crown in lieu of the salvage award to which it was legally entitled.

From the point of view of the Customs and Excise, however, the vital point was not ownership, but the payment of import duty. They regarded the *Amsterdam* in the same light as a ship that had just docked, and goods recovered from her must pass through Customs entry before they could be counted as officially 'imported', and thus legally present on British soil. The standard entry form for the barrel presented a nice problem, in that we could not say definitely what it contained without opening it, and inevitably risking destruction of the contents in the delays of the ensuing formalities. However, in view of the fact that there was no import duty actually payable on articles over one hundred years old, the Customs helpfully decided there was no legal need to give details of the contents.

Unfortunately, this 'hundred-year' rule did not include wine and spirits, so that a Customs officer had to come to our archaeological headquarters to inspect the dozen full bottles! On seeing their condition, he reported that, although they might contain a fluid chemically classifiable as wine, it was quite undrinkable, and that the imposition of import duty was unjustifiable. This was a relief since the Collier letters record that the ship contained 'many thousand dozen' such bottles, which would have added up to a total import duty sufficient to end the entire project!

Having dealt with the questions of legal ownership and import regulations, we were now to be confronted by the problems of export. The Export Licensing branch of the Department of Trade would not accept the view of Customs and Excise that the objects were 'imported' only when brought ashore in 1984, or that they could be treated as 'temporary imports' merely in transit to Holland. In their view the arrival of the objects in United Kingdom territorial waters in 1749 constituted their date of import, and that they were consequently subject to the Export Licensing Law designed to stop antiquities, works of art and documents from leaving the country if they were believed to be of outstanding importance.

In the case of the barrel, the conservators at Hastings had three times to take action, when the lead showed signs of deterioration, before a licence finally arrived on 19 November. And even then we were granted only a 'temporary licence', and had to make the barrel available for return to Britain by 31 January 1985 if required, by which date proof would have to be supplied to show that it did not contain some priceless object, such as a vase or painting, in addition to the animal fat.

Looking back on the excavation of 1984, however, it is not the problems but the fulfilment of all our hopes as to the ship itself that remain in the memory. Two thirds of the hull was again confirmed as remaining, and it still contained a substantial part of its cargo, as well as the equipment and personal possessions of both passengers and crew. The venture was proving richly worth while, and we looked forward eagerly to resuming further work.

12

Raising the Amsterdam

The success of the 1984 excavation meant that the excavation of the entire ship underwater could be considered as a serious alternative to the 'dry' excavation plan (entailing the enclosure of the site by a circular dyke), already proposed. We had anticipated that the diving skill of Jon Adams, Jerzy Gawronski, and the volunteers, would make it possible, but it had been a bonus to discover that there was good visibility of up to two or three metres at high tide, which enabled careful supervision of the operation, and recording of every stage. There would also be a major benefit, not only of reduced cost, but of being able to reduce the annual workload to manageable proportions by spreading it over a number of years, especially in the handling of the conservation of the mass of objects.

Whichever method should eventually be adopted, the recovery procedure for the ship will be the same. Many of the hull timbers will need to be refastened together as they are uncovered, and, once the interior is cleared, the pit in which the ship lies will be prepared for a particularly high tide. Large flotation tanks, capable of lifting the estimated 500 tonnes of the empty hull, would then probably be lowered and the ship made fast to them before they were pumped full of air to lift her from the bottom, in the same way as was done with the Swedish warship *Wasa*. She could then be towed to deeper water, where a large, submersible pontoon would be slipped beneath her, enabling her to be raised to the surface for the first time since 1749.

This method of transport on the deck of a pontoon had been effectively employed both in the case of the *Wasa*, and the nineteenth century iron ship *Great Britain*, the latter having been brought all the way from the Falkland Islands in the South Atlantic to her final resting place at Bristol in south-west England in this fashion. In comparison with such an epic voyage, the *Amsterdam*'s journey home, retracing the route of her maiden voyage two-

XXII. Sketch by Jon Adams (above) showing the *Amsterdam*'s stern structure as revealed in the careful excavation of 1984. Adjacent to the ship is the platform from which the excavation was carried out by divers. This contrasts with the serious damage caused by using mechanical excavators in the 1969 salvage operation. In the photograph (below) the end of the ship's fallen mast is being heaved up out of the beach until it broke.

and-a-half centuries earlier, should be comparatively simple. The greater problems might arise only in the final stage of her passage overland, after reaching Amsterdam, to the site where an exhibition hall and museum will need to be constructed round her.

The popular attraction of the *Amsterdam* for future visitors raises something of a problem for her restorers. Since the forecastle, quarter and poop decks of the ship are missing, we cannot know *exactly* what they were like. Yet, it would be wrong not to indicate their probable form. The specialist may be able to envisage the ship in her entirety in his mind's eye, but the layman needs to see her exactly as she was. Such points cannot be resolved in advance, but some have suggested that, rather than restore her with possible inaccuracy in wood, it might be better to follow the example of the incomplete Viking ships at Roskilde Museum, Denmark. There the form of the missing parts is indicated by an outline of metal strips. More satisfactory from the archaeological point of view maybe, but lacking in satisfaction for the ordinary visitor in the case of the much more complex construction of the East Indiaman.

Fortunately recent research in the archives of the Rijksmuseum and the Scheepvaart Museum in the Netherlands has thrown much fresh light on the general construction of the missing parts. Written descriptions, drawings, paintings, building plans, Company regulations, and ship models have filled the gaps to such a degree of certainty that a full-sized modern reconstruction of an eighteenth century East Indiaman is being made which, in combination with the original remains of the *Amsterdam* herself, will make it easy for everyone to visualise exactly what life was like aboard her.

It seems clear that there was little significant difference in the design and construction of the largest class of mid-eighteenth century Dutch East Indiamen. The exact form of some main features, such as the decorative wood carving of the stern, may vary from ship to ship, but a generally accurate reconstruction is possible. And, in the case of the *Amsterdam*, as I have already mentioned, we have been lucky enough even to have found part of the carving.

Vital to any such reconstruction in the case of the *Amsterdam* was an accurate knowledge of her knee timbers. In the case of the upper gun deck – the feature we had identified as visible at beach level – the deck surface was mostly missing. However, if we recorded the spacing of the surviving knees which held the deck beams, then we could reconstruct much of the missing deck, for it was the knees which governed the position of the hatches, masts and capstan. Happily, with the *Amsterdam*, we could see not only the massive angled knee timbers (grown and cut to shape for maximum strength) which held the deck beams to the inside of the ship, but also the ends of some of the deck beams themselves. The traditional shape of oak trees, with short thick stem and great branches spreading horizontally, owes as much to craft as to nature, the trees being grown by selection and spacing to provide curved timbers for use without a joint to support the gun decks of wooden armed merchant ships and men-of-war. Each deck beam was held on one side by a 'hanging knee', and on the other by a 'lodging knee', the latter being a small angled timber lying horizontally, which was attached both to the inside of the hull and to the side of each deck beam.

It is clear that the foremost quarter of the surviving part of the upper gun deck once underlay the forecastle, itself a short deck, and it was on this section of the upper deck, probably on the port side, that the ship's galley was situated. Not only was all food cooked here, but the ship's cook and his mates made in their home. After the wreck of the ship and the destruction of most of the upper deck by the would-be salvors, many of the typical yellow clay Dutch bricks which lined the galley hearth fell onto the lower deck, where they were found in 1969, still retaining traces of the buff mortar once used to join them together.

The forecastle has a commanding position overlooking the ship's waist aft, and the head forward. It was a fairly unencumbered area, surrounded by a low guard rail, but the foremast came up through the middle of it, and also the box-like chimney leading up from the galley hearth on the deck below. The pride of the forecastle was the ship's bronze bell, which was hung in a special cage at the after edge, where it was in full view of the men working on the upper gun deck in the ship's waist. It is the greatest of pities that all trace of this forecastle seems to have disappeared.

Looking forward, a visitor standing on the forecastle would have looked down onto the head of the ship, a kind of platform projecting out over the sea on either side of the bowsprit. Here were the toilets for the ordinary seaman and senior ratings. This platform rested upon the 'knee of the head', and although it was long ago destroyed, the supporting knee survives. Attached to the forward side of the stempost, it is composed of a series of wedge-shaped timbers bolted together. A special cutwater timber lies on the leading edge of the knee, the forward face of which we found to have a lead sheathing, and although the upper part has either rotted away or fallen off, we know that this was the support for the ship's figurehead. Although the figurehead, probably a lion, is missing; it is by no means certain that it is lost since it may have fallen into the soft clay beside the bow. The knee of the head was held in position also by two small horizontal knees on each side, holding the head to the side of the hull: these were each known as a 'cheek of the head'. At the time of our first examination of the ship, substantial portions of the lower of each of these still remained in position, but since then they have most regrettably been hacked away by irresponsible souvenir hunters, who neither cared nor appreciated the very considerable damage they were doing. Fortunately, however, I have a good photographic and drawn record of the now missing lower cheek timbers. The knee of the head also has traces of two notches cut in it, which must have been for holding ropes attached to the bowsprit, and probably to the foremast, for similar holes in similar positions also appear on contemporary ship models.

From the surviving height of the knee of the head, it seems that the knee was placed rather higher up the stempost than was normal, though this need not have significantly raised the level of the head platform where the toilets lay. The crew's quarters were on the lower gun deck, and to reach the 'heads' they would have had to walk to the forward end of the deck, and climb up steps onto the upper gun deck just forward of the galley, and then to open a door leading out onto the platform. The toilets themselves were flat wooden seats on box-like wooden chutes overlying the sea, and although a visit to the 'heads' was no doubt a pleasure in good weather, it is known that other less hygienic and more unofficial places inside the ship were used in rough weather. Chamber pots were a godsend on board ship, which is why they were often found in the debris of old wooden shipwrecks, but even they had to be emptied and cleaned from time to time. When men were lying on the lower deck sick and dying, as were so many in the *Amsterdam*, there was every incentive not to use the 'heads'. The higher ranks also preferred the use of a chamber pot on occasion, and one of pewter was recovered from the 1743 wreck of the Dutch East Indiaman *Hollandia* off the Isles of Scilly.

Steps led down from the forecastle onto the upper gun deck in the ship's waist, and this was the only part of this deck which lay open to the weather. Here the ship's company mustered for daily prayers, sick parade, orders, and floggings. The main mast stood at the after end of the waist, and just forward of it lay the main hatch leading down through the lower deck into the hold. The special arrangement of the deck beams in the *Amsterdam* necessary to hold the main mast is reflected by the surviving knees on each side of the ship which once held them in place, so that we can with a fair degree of confidence reconstruct the position of the main mast, and also the main hatch, on this deck.

The extent of the waist can also be defined, for all the ship models show that the wooden shelves (called 'channels') projecting from each side of the ship, which once held the lower ends of the shrouds – the ropes keeping the masts upright – extended usually to the after end of the forecastle. These 'channels' have been destroyed, but the iron bolts which once held the port side foremast channel to the side of the ship are still in the hull, and so both give an exact idea of its extent, and enable us to estimate where the after edge of the forecastle came. The after end of the waist can be deduced with reasonable accuracy, since the position of the main mast and main hatch are known.

At the after end of the ship's waist were the steps leading up onto the quarter deck, but if, instead of clambering up, one continued walking aft along the upper gun deck, the ship's capstan would be found just abaft the main mast. Nobody yet knows if any part of this massive revolving drum used for hauling in the anchor survives, but in view of its great weight and the fact that it rested on a special timber construction on the lower deck, it is likely still to be there, at least in part. Even if it should have disappeared, however, its position will be clearly indicated by the abnormal placing of the knees which would once have held the upper deck beams which in turn kept the capstan steady.

Small cabins were ranged along each side of the upper gun deck close to the capstan, and it was here that the *Amsterdam*'s five passengers were lodged. Further aft were the cabins of the officers, and at the stern their mess room, with its pleasant outlook through the stern windows. At this stage it is impossible to tell if any trace of these cabins survives, but some clues may remain on the port side of the ship where a little of the flooring of the upper gun deck does survive.

The quarter deck above overlay about half of the upper gun deck, and it was from here that Captain Willem Klump and his First Lieutenant sang out the orders to their crew in the curious Dutch fashion. Here, too, Klump must have paced up and down during the gale, keeping a weather eye on the mountainous seas crashing over the gunwale into the waist, and knowing full well that it was more or less impossible to tack a zig-zag course against a south-westerly gale. I wonder how many times he gripped the curving handrail and, looking down at the scurrying sailors trying to dodge the next torrent of surging water, cursed the confusion the gale had brought to his new ship.

It was further aft on the quarter deck that there existed the nerve centre of the ship. Immediately behind the mizzen mast lay the large spoked wheel for steering the ship, and just behind that the captain's quarters, the roof of which formed the poop deck. Willem Klump's quarters would have reflected his personal tastes and may have contained items of his own furniture. Judging from models of eighteenth century Dutch East Indiamen, he probably slept in a special small cabin on one side of the deck, from which a small barred window enabled him to see down forward into the quarter deck. His sleeping cabin door opened onto a short passage, across which lay another cabin, also with an iron-barred window, and here the treasure chests were probably locked away. At the after end of these quarters, opening out from the end of the passageway, was the ship's great cabin where the officers and passengers joined him for meals. It was here that Klump probably first established acquaintance with Andries van Bockom and his wife Pieternella, in the weeks that the *Amsterdam* was weatherbound at Texel. We can imagine them chatting over a glass of red wine before dinner, while watching through the great stern windows the arriving ships in this busy waterway into the heart of Holland.

Alas, the quarter deck and the poop deck are gone, and with them the decorated stern. Eighteenth century decoration is restrained compared with the magnificence of the preceding century, but the stern would still have undoubtedly been finely carved and painted. We can be sure of two features: the coat of arms of the City of Amsterdam (three white crosses on a central black zone on a red shield) and the name of the ship, probably on an elaborate scroll. The rest of it may always remain a mystery in the case of the *Amsterdam*, but the revelation in the excavation of 1984 that on the port quarter the bottom of the decoration had been carved in the form of a fishtail provides a valuable clue. This is important since the VOC Book-keeper's record for the carving has been found at The Hague, and shows that the work on the stern was executed by Jan Hogendijk and Co. for 380 guilders, and that the firm also worked on the *Oudcarspel* and the *Schuylenburgh* at approximately the same date, so that further research may discover examples of their style of work for the Amsterdam chamber of the VOC.

The figurehead was probably a lion, either gilded or painted yellow, not only because this was the most popular single subject for a ship's figurehead at the time, but because the lion was the heraldic beast of Holland.

The excavation of 1984 also confirmed that a substantial part of the lower gun deck survived. The forward area was shared by the crew with the massive twelve-pound cannons, among which they slung their hammocks. The rear was often partitioned off for occupation by the non-commissioned officers, and it was found that they also kept the 'tools of their trade' there. Amongst the ramrods for guns was a gunner's tally stick, and even barrels of musket balls and a group of musket cartridge belts still carefully wrapped up together, which seems to show the exact area where the Constapel or Master Gunner, Floris de Vos of Amsterdam, had his quarters.

Exactly what lies below the lower gun deck can only be discovered by further excavation, but several mid-eighteenth century VOC ship drawings have been found which show in detail what we may expect. They include deck plans, sections, and construction details from the yard of Pieter van Zwijndregt Pzn, a master shipwright of Rotterdam, preserved in the Prins Hendrik Museum there. By a remarkable coincidence they are for the 140 ft *Noordt Nieuwlandt*, built in 1750, only two years after the *Amsterdam*. As compared with British ships of that date, the *Amsterdam* would have a fairly flat bottom, and there is probably a row of vertical stanchions along the middle line of her hold. There is probably also a short orlop deck just inside the bow, as well as just inside the stern, to take the ship's stores and food supply. In fact one of William Press's excavators seems to have reached down to the deck at the bow to recover some of the stores, but fortunately the cargo itself doesn't seem to have been disturbed.

Once the excavation is complete and the ship returned home, many of those who will eventually visit her will be fascinated by the experience of stepping back for a brief while into the past, and I have never in fact talked to anyone about the *Amsterdam* without finding their imagination fired by some aspect of her, but when the visit is over and the postcards and the souvenirs are bought, there may come a moment when perhaps a reaction may dominate. 'All right, I was interested. Walking on that deck and seeing all those things, just as I'd have walked and seen them if I had been alive two hundred years ago. But, when it comes down to it, and though I wouldn't have missed the experience, it doesn't have much significance or relevance to what's going on today. It is all just dead and gone.'

I can sympathise with this feeling, and had it in mind myself in the spring of 1972 when, with a research grant from the Dutch Ministry of Culture, I boarded a KLM jet at London Airport for the first time to retrace the voyage of the *Amsterdam*. From high over the North Sea, I looked down upon the course of the ship until the aircraft rushed inland over the colourful patchwork quilt of Holland's bulb fields, and minutes later landed at Amsterdam's Schiphol Airport, having made the air journey from London in a comfortable forty minutes in contrast to the fatal two months the *Amsterdam* took to reach the English shore.

It was here in the beautiful old city of Amsterdam that I came to understand better and appreciate the ship on which we had been working for so long, and to see its relationship to modern Dutch society. As a tangible link with that vital age in Dutch history when the country burst from the bonds of Spanish rule to assert itself as one of the most influential of modern European nations, the ship was an embodiment of the spirit of enterprise which made the Netherlands the great trading nation she still is. Walking along the old quays amidst the merchant houses, I saw the *Amsterdam* less in isolation than as one of the great series of ships which had set sail from here, and remembered that one of her namesakes, a much earlier *Amsterdam*, had been among the first four ships which formed the initial Dutch venture in the Indies trade. Indeed there is a plaque set up in Amsterdam, which records this event. The fleet had sailed in 1595 for a special trading organisation, the Company van Verre, and had met with but indifferent success, but a pattern had been laid down, and in another few years more ships followed. This time the harvest was richer, and the Dutch East India Company was born.

Even though the Company itself passed from history upon its bankruptcy in 1798–9, it has left lasting traces of its existence not only in the Netherlands, but abroad. On my very first day in Amsterdam, the many Indonesian restaurants and the numerous Indonesian people in the streets provided live evidence of the former VOC empire. Traditions have remained unbroken here for three centuries, and when I went down to the site of the Company shipbuilding yard where the *Amsterdam* had been shaped upon the stocks, I found a firm called 'Stork Werkspoor' operating there – manufacturing marine engines. The firm has, in fact, its own private museum and the curator, Mr van Hoffen, took me over it to see the carefully preserved relics of VOC days. It was strange to stand where the *Amsterdam* had had her birth, and beyond the smell of engine oil and welded metal, perhaps a hint of tar and wood shavings lingered.

It is a source of delighted wonder for visitors to see how well the beautiful homes of the wealthy seventeenth- and eighteenth-century merchants have survived the years and have been expertly restored. Sound as their ships they still stand as a memorial, not to a fattening on the richness of their own land, but to their creation by their own ability of a Golden Age in a country without great natural resources. As we have seen, it was created at considerable human costs, but the humane structure of modern Dutch society would be the poorer without that foundation. This is one of the main legacies of the VOC, but there are others in modern South Africa and Indonesia, which would not have developed in the way that they have without the quickening activities of the VOC. Here also there has been a human cost, but we shall not understand the histories of these countries without a consciousness of the contribution made to their growth by the Company, and how this in turn has modified the relationships which govern international dealings in the modern world.

For Britain, too, the story of the VOC has an importance. It was through the Company's exports all over Europe that the expertise of Dutch merchants in their choice of goods and products influenced the way of life of the whole of the Continent, and their methods influenced trading practice there throughout the seventeenth and eighteenth centuries. In particular the rivalry with the Dutch modified part of Britain's own trading pattern in the past, and in part caused Britain to develop India as the centre of its trading empire in the Far East.

Holland had rivals in her East Indies trade, especially Britain, Denmark, France and Portugal, so that the *Amsterdam* belongs to a class of ship which did much to open up trade on a global scale. However, there is no other known survivor among the East Indiamen of any nation which has a reasonably well preserved hull fitted out for the long voyage to the Far East.

Even today the Netherlands is an extremely important trading nation, with an influence out of all proportion to her small size. It seems particularly fitting, therefore, that the Netherlands has been gifted with the splendid opportunity of choosing a merchant ship as the representation of her seagoing heritage. Scaled down to manageable size within the structure of a single ship and her cargo, all the aspects of that heritage are illustrated, and brought home to us through the emerging story of a group of people whose lives were for a short time bound up in her.

APPENDIX A

English Records

The 'Collier Letters'

1.

Letter from Mr Thomas Smith, Custom House Officer at Eastbourne to his brother-in-law, Mr Collier, Agent to the Duke of Newcastle.
Dated January 17th, 1748. (Jan. 28, 1749 N.S.) (*2 days after wreck.*)

Thear is a large Dutch Ship a Shore a bout half a mille to the east of Bullverhithe, which I hope it will not be trouble some to give you a short account off, her names the Amsterdam, of Amsterdam, bound to Batavia in the East Indies burden a bout 600 or 700 tons, 333 men, 54 guns, Capt. Williams Klump Commander, haveing on board 28 chest of silver, of which 27 are lodg'd in the custom house, but what value in each chest is unknown, but sume of them is as much as two men can carry, and this affter noon one barrel is brought to the custom house full of silver, and I think as heavy as any of the chests; the one chest as was missing is since found, but emty, the rest of her cargo in particular can not learn, but in general they answer, all sort of goods – they have been at Sea 2 months, in which time have lost 50 men by sickness, and several more have died since the ship as been a shore. She came in Sunday 3 a clock in the affter noon, while the people was at Church, with fireing a great many guns. The rest of the news of the town I leave to my wife, and so conclude with the sincearest wishes for your recoverey and safe return home: and I am your Most Obedient and Humble Sart.

Thos. Smith

Postscript. The Capt. (Klump) Sett out for London this morning.

2.

Letter from Mrs Smith to Mr Collier.
Dated January 17th, 1748. (Jan. 28, 1749, N.S.) (*2 days after wreck.*)

We have had great feasting. I have been in vited to all but I did not go to any, but thay have beter bisness at present for thar Is all sorts of good things to be got at the rack (wreck). I have not seen any thing that came out of her as yet. There is 3 Ladies and thay do say 2 of them ar very fine women. Thay are at the Maidenhead and have drink tea at Mr. Coppards [at the Custom House].
. . . . We have had very bad wether and ye waters very much over flod every wear.

3.

Letter to Mr Collier from Mr George Worge his son-in-law.
Dated January 17th, 1748. (January 28, 1749, N.S.) (*2 days after wreck.*)

We have had for a long time past the most terrible wheather that I ever remember, and Sunday last in the afternoon a Dutch East Indiaman was drove a shore at Bulverhith, & yesterday I rode down to see her, & from one of her officers who spoke a little English I had this acct, that she was called the Amsterdam, of that place, & bound for Batavia, abt 700 tuns & 52 guns, & had when she came out abt two Months agoe three hundred men, abt halfe of w'ch had been lost by sickness & washed over board, & loaded with money, bale goods, & stores of all kinds. She was a new ship, & had been all this time beating abt & and never got beyond Beachy in her way. She Struck in Pevensy Bay & lost her rudder, & has laid off Bexhill at anchor severall day's. Some of the Hastings people got to her, & undertook to carry her to Portsmouth when the wheather would permit, but she could hold out no longer than Sunday.

She stands in a good place, & in appearance quite whole, & may do so for some months, But no possibility of getting her off. I Believe they will save every thing that is worth saveing, to the great disappointm't of the wreckers who come from all parts of the country for plunder, there was yesterday when I was there more than a thousand of these wretches with long poles & hooks at the Ends.

But all the soldiers on the coast are there, & behave well at present – they keep the country people off, & their officers keep the soldiers to rights. They have carried to the Custom house at Hasting 27 chests of money, & other pt of her ladeing will be carried to Hastings as fast as it can be got out. One chest was emptied of its money by somebody, and, as it's said, was so before it came out of the ship. But it's gone, & by whome is not known.

I could get no certain acct of the quantity of money, some said three-score thousand pounds, others made it a great deal more, & others much less. The value of the Ship & cargoe as uncertain, but two hundred thousand pounds was the generall estimate. There was three women on board, who are now at Hasting. When I was down there were then abt forty sick men in the ship, w'ch they afterwards got out & sent to Hasting. I saw Sir Chs. Eversfield there, who told me he was down when she came on Shore, & that all the crew were drunk, & so were all of them that I saw yesterday.

4.

Letter from Mr Richard Patrick to Mr Collier.
Dated January 24th, 1748. (4 February, 1749, N.S.) (*9 days after wreck.*)

The Dutch Ship I have mentioned to you still sits whole, and the plunderers speed but very indifferently, neither do the Owners save any quantity of goods, for the Ship is so much Swerved in the Sand, that it is impossible to get at the cargoe, the Ship being always full of water.

Mr. Whitfield is down, & is the Chief Manager at this wreck. The Ship is not on Shore in the Liberty of Hasting, and the soldiers have shot a man indiscretely at this wreck, and Mr. Tilden, as Coroner for the Rape of Hasting, has been apply'd to upon the affair, to summons a jury to view the body and to enquire into the death of this p'son, but as Mr. Tilden is laid up with a fit of the gout, he desired me to act as his deputy, upon which I went over to Battell to him, and consulted him thereupon, as likewise Mr. Worge, who both joyn'd in opinion with me, that the death of this p'son was not to be enquired into by the Coroner and jury, by reason he was kild at sea, ten or fifteen roads below highwater Mark. Mr. Worg also informed me he should write to you by the last post, and that he would mention to you the affair of the death of this unfortunate person.

5.

Letter from Mr Richard Patrick to Mr Collier.
Dated January 31st, 1748. (11 February, 1749, N.S.) (*16 days after wreck.*)

I reced your last without date, and will take care to seize the best anchor & cable belonging to the Dutch ship stranded near Bulverhith.

The ship is really a meloncholy sight to behold, for she lyes on shore, upon a boggy sand, that she is swerved almost as high as her Upper Deck, and notwithstanding all the contrivances imagineable, the main hatches can't be open'd, so that it's feared most part of the cargoe in the main hold will perish in the sand.

They have endeavoured to burn the decks, and have made a bone fire thereupon, which had no effect, notwithstanding they burnt, at one time, two hundred batt faggots. They have also endeavoured to blow up the decks with gun powder, but as the ship is so much swerved, she always continues under water, that they can't fix barrels of powder at a proper place for that purpose.

Upon the ships coming on shore, I waited on Mr. Coppard, & the Captain, in relation to makeing a Protest. It seems the super cargoe had drawn a Protest before they came on shore, which was signed by the Captain & all the Officers, which was shewn to Mr. Mayor, who thinks the same sufficient, as the Capt. &c. has sworn the contents thereof before him to be true, so that I have not in the least been concern'd in the unhappy affair only that I have been twice to see the ship in this unfortunate scituation.

As Mr. Cramp is an Assistant at this wreck, & is always present when there is anything to be done, and as he has a deputation from the Duke of Newcastle, I have desired him to secure the best anchor & cable for His Grace, who has promised me to take all possible care therein. Last Friday night we had abundance of snow, and yesterday was a very rainy day which has in great measure consumed the same. This day is like to prove fair but extremely cold.

Postscript. There was a chest of silver broke open the night the ship came on shore, by some of our town gentm, containing a great quantity of wedges of silver, weighing about 5 pound each wedge, the whole value amounting to about £1200 Sterling. On Mr. Whitfields arrival he had it cry'd round the town, if any p'son or p'sons who had taken any of these wedges of silver and wou'd bring the same to him, they shou'd have forty shillings pr. wedge, & no questions asked, otherwise in case they were found guilty, they wou'd be severely punished. Several of these silver-wedges have been delivered to Mr. Whitfield, but am afraid he will never be able to get the whole, as a great many of those fellows carry such vile principals, for had not several of these creatures offered the silver for sale, I question whether this affair wou'd have been discovered.

6.

Letter from Dr Russel to Mr Collier.
Dated 6th February, 1748. (17 February, 1749, N.S.) (*22 days after wreck.*)

It seems Hastings is now ye scene of a most considerable wreck. Ye town repository of money by chests full and that our neighbour is there taking care of ye effects for ye owners.

7.

Letter from Mr George Worge from Battle to Mr Collier at Bath.
Dated 11th February, 1748. (22 February, 1749, N.S.) (*27 days after wreck.*)

I would send you News, but really we have none – the wreck ingrosses all, & this you must have heard so much of to be tired with it – so shall only say that, either from the want of skill or honesty of the agent or managers, there is very little done towards getting out & saveing the cargoe. They blew up part of one of the decks this morning . . .

8.

Letter from Mr Thorpe, Mayor of Hastings, to Mr Collier.
Dated February 22nd, 1748. (5 March, 1749, N.S.) (*38 days after wreck.*)

I doubt not but you have had successive accounts of the Dutch ship run ashore near Bulverhith, since which the care of the sick Dutchmen, the plague of quartering soldiers, their & others thieving, has engrossed my whole time. This happening so soon after the Nympha [*La Nympha Americana*, a Spanish vessel, was wrecked November 29th, 1747, at Birling Gap] has destroyed the morals & honesty of too many of our country men, for the very people hired to save did little else but steal. The Hoo people came in a body, and carried off velvett, cloth, &c. but on warrants being issued, they submit to deliver all again. One of them stopped a waggon, & called others to his assistance to rob it. I committed him to goal, & have since gott Mr. Nicoll to take the examinations again, and he has made his Mittimus for Horsham.

The treasure of the ship, amounting to near thirty thousand pounds value, being sent to London has eased us of a Company of Foot, who were the greatest thieves I ever knew, they not only robbed at the ship, but their quarters also. The Dutch soldiers & sailors robed their Officers, as did too many of our own town.

There was a chest containing fifty Wedges of silver each, weighing about four pounds & a half, broke open the first night, but by one means or another we have recovered thirty six, & a gold watch, but a very little of the gold & silver lace and wearing apparel. There are some cables & anchors, some provisions, as butter, bacon, beef, &c. saved, also several chest of wine in bottles, of which there is in the ship a great many thousand dozen.

The ship is so swerved in the sand, that at high water the sea covers her, and at low, her lower Deck is under water. They have endeavoured to blow up her decks with gunpowder, sometimes succeeding, at others not, the powder being obliged to be putt under water, but this morning they blew up a great part of the lower deck, and its thought the composition next the match being too dry, fired so quick, that Mr. Nutt the Engineer perished . . .

P.S. The wine is French – if you would have any, please to let me know, I fancy about 1 shilling a bottle will be the price.

Newspaper Extract

An extract from some contemporary paper not named by Mr Brett and dated Feb. 23rd (5th March, 1749, N.S.) or a day or two earlier. (*39 days after wreck.*) He refers to it as 'a paragraph in our *Collectanea*' which reads thus:

'The Engineer engaged to blow up a portion of the *Amsterdam* at Bulverhithe is himself blown to pieces through letting the fuse go off too soon. The ship is not more than half unloaded, nor can the work be further proceeded with until the timbers are shattered, the work of which it is said will be again attempted on March 6th. [17 March, 1749, N.S.]'

The name of the unfortunate Engineer [adds Mr Brett] was Christopher Nutt, and the St Clement's Register shows that his remains were placed in the churchyard of that parish.

APPENDIX B

'The Payroll of Outward-Bound Fair – Christmas – and Easter Ships 1748/49'

by Joop Reinboud

A remarkable book is hidden behind the catalogue number K.A. 9549 of the Colonial Archives in The Hague. It is the earliest of seven big volumes, the only ones to survive of all the land payrolls of the Dutch East India Company during the whole of its existence, originally more than 190 in number! This particular volume deals with the fleets of 1748/9, and lists the names of everyone on board the outward-bound East Indiamen, noting their presence or absence at the time the register was taken, whether they were suffering from any illness, etc., and also the amount of the two months pay due in advance to each member of the crew before his ship left Texel.

In fact each ship also carried two ship payrolls when it sailed for Batavia. These gave a full *curriculum vitae* of all the ship's company, complete with details of dates and places, and recording all sums paid over to them, and so on. One copy was retained in the Company archives in the Indies, and the other was sent back to Amsterdam.

After the *Amsterdam* ran ashore at Hastings in January 1749, these ship payrolls were lost, so that the only account of those aboard for this unfortunate maiden voyage appears in the volume numbered KA 9549 in the Kolonial Archief, and inscribed 'Betaals rolle van de uitgaande Kermis – Kerst – en Paasschepen 1748/49' – Payroll of Outward-Bound Fair – Christmas – and Easter Ships 1748/49. The title indicates the time of the fleet sailings to the Far East: the autumn – the time of the Fairs; the end of the year – about Christmas; and the spring – Easter-time, with an extension into summer. The vellum binding bears the names of all the ships for this particular year, and among them the *Amsterdam*.

Since there were 333 persons aboard her, and the payroll gives scrupulous details of each, it is impossible to include it in the present book, but even a summarised list is useful in showing what a varied cross-section of European life, the ship's company represents. Set apart at the head of the list are the three women passengers, and it was in the space between their names and the beginning of the list of higher rank male maritime employees – which included van Bockom – that a later hand inserted the brief notice of the *Amsterdam*'s fate. Ranging from the captain himself to the ship's cooks and carpenters, there were 39 of these specially skilled men, and one appointee. Next came 87 men, the crews of the ship's guns, who were subdivided according to their rate of pay into three classes. Many of these were what we might call 'able seamen' or gun captains, while in addition there were 18 ordinary seamen, 20 juniors, 23 apprentices, and at the very bottom of the pile, 3 ship's boys. These are followed by the 11 artisans who were presumably intended for the Company's shore establishments and the military complement of five officers and 123 soldiers. It is interesting to note that almost 80 per cent of the recruited men came from the German countries, less than 15 per cent of these soldiers being drawn from the Netherlands itself.

The rendering of the men's names by the payroll clerk was phonetic, and not even consistently so. Even the *Amsterdam*'s commander, Captain lieutenant Willem Klump, has his name written 'Clump' when he is recorded as having gone bail for ship's boy Jacob Baks (No. 188), though in the very next entry over the page, in respect of the boy Adrianus Welgevaren, the spelling reverts to Klump. Most of the names of the foreigners aboard, and they were in the majority, were 'translated' into Dutch. Able seaman Wilkes of Harrier (No. 49), who may have been an Englishman, probably answered to the names John Henry, but he is listed as Jan Hendrik! Curiously enough, he had an exact namesake in a slightly lower grade, but the other Jan Hendrik Wilkes (No. 93) hailed from Cuxhaven. Names of countries and towns were similarly treated, but generally remain recognisable, and have been allowed to stand.

Naturally, in a long maritime tradition, there developed names for special ranks within the ship's company which are very difficult to render exactly in English, but some indication of function has been given to make the terms more intelligible. A prime example is that of the *ziekentrooster*, already discussed in the text, and the daunting-looking *busschieter*, which actually translates very simply as 'blunderbuss-shooter' or 'gun-shot'. Even more strange to us is the concept of the 'bail', the person who would stand surety for the soldier or sailor in question, and who might – as in the entry given here for Pasmooij, the *ziekentrooster* – be a relative, but who was more frequently a professional moneylender, the same names recurring time and again. In return for advancing money to buy the cheap outfit these men needed for the voyage, a much larger sum was exacted by these 'bails', which was paid to them by the Company on behalf of the men concerned, who worked months or even years to earn enough to repay this debt. Such pledges or 'schedules', for which the Dutch word is 'ceels', were in themselves an article of trade, and were freely bought and sold. Consequently, the moneylenders were known as *ceel*-sellers, or, because of the similarity of the Dutch word for 'soul' *ziel*, as *ziel*-sellers – *zielverkoopers*. An Amsterdam tax-register, *Personele Quotisatie* of 1742 shows only one man, Joost Duijff, specifically referred to as a *zielverkooper*, and interestingly enough, his name occurs in the payroll entries for a number of the soldiers aboard the *Amsterdam* – Nos. 316, 320, 321 and 322. On the other hand eight men listed in the tax register as 'innkeepers' are named as 'bails' in the payroll, thus illustrating the point made in the text that the *volkhouders* who provided the men with 'board and lodging' during their period of waiting to join their ship continued as their 'bails' to prey on their earnings once they were aboard.

Pre-eminent among those with whom the men on the *Amsterdam* ran up debts however, is J(an) Jansz or Janssoon, to whom a total of 4,375 guilders was owed, although he appears in the tax-register as a boat-builder or timber merchant. The runner-up is a man called Scholte, to whom 2,250 guilders were owed, and who may possibly be the Jan Scholte whom the register describes as a wealthy merchant.

One of the mysteries of the *Amsterdam* concerns the quantity of goods for private trade brought aboard by members of the ship's company. Willem Klump and others had borrowed large sums of money to be repaid immediately on arrival at the Cape of Good Hope or in Batavia, so that they must have had a considerable amount of such trade goods with them. The Paybook makes no mention of them, however, and merely lists the number of *kists*, or chests, of personal belongings, and the number of chests or 'cellars' of wine bottles – *kelders* – which they had. Since the private trade was entirely 'unofficial' this is not surprising, and it seems that only during the future excavation of the ship may we find the answer as to what articles of trade Klump and the others were counting on to make their fortunes.

The payroll volume opens with a list of the ships of 1748–9 which sailed 'seaward from Texel' – *Uyt Texel in Zee*. The *Amsterdam* comes second, possibly reflecting her original placing among the ships due to sail in the later autumn, although her final sailing date – 18 January 1749 – is incorrectly given. The leaves are numbered in sequence, each leaf consisting of a closely-filled *recto* and *verso*, and the same number covering both sides of the sheet. The numbers appended to the names are given for convenience of reference, and are not in the original.

The opening page of the *Amsterdam*'s payroll reads as follows:

AMSTERDAM *Lang 150 Voeten*
AMSTERDAM: Length 150 feet

a   *Maria Monk Huysvr, vanden Luytenant Hal*   *Vry van kost & Transportgelt*
Maria Monk, wife of Lieutenant Hall   (No. 203). Free board and passage.

b   *Anna Pieternella Schook van Aernhem* ⎫   *huysvrouwe en Dienstmaagt van*
c   *Catharina Susanna Schook* ⎭   *de Heer Onder Cooperman Mr. Andreas van Boccum*

Anna Pieternella Schook of Arnhem ⎫   wife and maidservant of Junior
Catharina Susanna Schook ⎭   Merchant Andreas van Boccum LL.D.

Gebleeven Op de Cust van Sussex tusschen Hastings en Beachyhead gestrand
Perished. Run Aground on the Coast of Sussex between Hastings and Beachey Head

Willem Klump v Mittouw Capiteijn Luytenant   *f72/f114*
geen kist 5 kelders
Willem Klump of Mittau Captain Lieutenant   72 guilders per month
no chest, 5 cellars   144 paid in advance

2   *Mr. Andries van Bockom v Delft Ondr. Koopman*   *f40/f80*
3 kisten 5 kelders
Mr Andries van Bockom of Delft Junior Merchant   40 guilders per month
3 chests, 5 cellars   80 guilders due in advance

3   *Cornelis Pasmooij van Amsterdam Ziekentrooster*   *f24/f48*
Maria Bosman inde Madelivestraat over de
Slootstraat Uytdraagster
d f 300 aan J. Jans 3 m aan ziin vrouw Maria Bosman
te Amsterdam
1 kist 4 kelders
Cornelis Pasmooij of Amsterdam Sick-visitor. His   24 guilders per month
bail was his wife Maria Bosman who lived in   48 due in advance
Madelivenstraat (Daisy Street) in Amsterdam, and
was a secondhand dealer. He was indebted for 300
guilders to J. Jans, and three months of his wages
are to be paid to his wife, the said Maria Bosman of
Amsterdam.
1 chest, 4 cellars

182

To continue the list in summarised form with the reverse of the first leaf dealing with the *Amsterdam*, folio 37 v.:

					f	f
	4	Martinus van den Hoet	s' Graveland	Luytenant (Lieutenant)	48	96
	5	Jurriaan Bartels	Sonderburg	Onder Stuurman (Second Mate)	32	64
	6	Jan Kwast	Amsterdam	Derdewaak (Third Mate)	26	52
	7	Jan Spek	Amsterdam	Derdewaak (Third Mate)	26	52
fo. 38	8	Jan Fredrik Rippen	Breemen	Bootsman (Boatswain)	22	44
	9	Jacob van der Linden	Breukelen	Bootsmansmaat (Boatswain's mate)	14	28
	10	Paulus Dreijer	de Leep	Schieman (Rigger)	20	40
	11	Jacobus Boekhout	Amsterdam	Schiemansmaat (Rigger's mate)	14	28
	12	Gerrit Berlaage	Amsterdam	Bottelier (Steward)	20	40
fo. 38 v.	13	Jacobus Nieuwburg	Amsterdam	Botteliersmaat (Understeward)	14	28
	14	Floris de Vos	Amsterdam	Constapel (Master Gunner)	22	44
	15	Fredrik Willem van Vas	Amersfoort	Constapelsmaat (Master Gunner's mate)	14	28
	16	Sijmen de Leeuw	Amsterdam	Constapelsmaat (Master Gunner's mate)	14	28
fo. 39	17	Christiaan Bruijn	Yena	Kok (Cook)	20	40
	18	Lambertus Schutjens	Valkenburg	Koksmaat (Cook's mate)	14	28
	19	Ary Mes	Hilversum	Quartiermeester (Quartermaster)	14	28
	20	Frans Hendrik Beekman	Renkhoesen	Quartiermeester		

			(Quartermaster)	14	28
	21 Henderik Exterkort	Amsterdam	Quartiermeester (Quartermaster)	14	28
fo. 39 v.	22 Jan de Bruijn	Amsterdam	Quartiermeester (Quartermaster)	12	24
	23 Pieter Wiltschut	Amsterdam	Opperzylemaker (Sailmaker)	20	40
	24 Mechiel Cornelisz Waak	Amsterdam	Onderzylemaker (Sailmaker's mate)	14	28
	25 Jan Michiel Wiggeri	Hamburg	Opper Kuyper (Cooper)	16	32
	26 Jan de Ruijter	Amsterdam	Onderkuyper (Copper's mate)	14	28
fo. 40	27 Mechiel van Beeg	Delft	Onderkuyper (Cooper's mate)	14	28
	28 Christoffel Izak Wilman	Holstyn	Scheepscorporaal (Ship's Corporal)	14	28
	29 Cornelis Martensz	Scherwoude	Provoost (Provost, with custody of offenders)	12	24
	30 Machiel Flaming	Hamburg	Trompetter (Trumpeter)	16	32
	31 Hendrik Christiaan Brumleij	Saxen Lauwen- burg	Opper Meester (Surgeon)	36	108
fo. 40 v.	32 Willem Buijs	Amsterdam	Tweede Meester (Surgeon's mate)	22	44
	33 Jan Matthys Gregory Matthysz	Amsterdam	Derde Meester (Surgeon's Second mate)	14	28
	34 Jan Christiaan	Hamburg	Oppertimmerman (Carpenter)	48	96
	35 Hendrik Kuijper	Amsterdam	Ondertimmerman (Carpenter's mate)	34	68

	36	Cornelis van Anraat	Utrecht	Ondertimmerman (Carpenter's mate)	30 60
fo. 41	37	Uuldrik Myndersz	Amsterdam	Ondertimmerman (Carpenter's mate)	24 48
	38	Dominicus Jansz	Amsterdam	Ondertimmerman (Carpenter's mate)	24 48
	39	Carl Meijer	Amsterdam	Ondertimmerman (Carpenter's mate)	16 32

APPOINTEES

fo. 41 v.	40	Gerrit Voorn	Amsterdam		10 20

fo. 42

BUSSCHIETERS *a f 12*

(Gun captains at 12 guilders a month)

	41	Jacob Hantz	Hoesem	12	24
	42	Christoffel Jasper	Dreringen	12	24
	43	Christiaan Andriesz	Aalburg	12	24
	44	Jan Dirksz	Carelskroon	12	24
	45	Claas Steen	Elmshoorn	12	24
	46	Christoffel Paulusz	Oland	12	24
	47	Laurens Sunders	Bergen op Zoom	12	24
	48	Jacob Groenewout	Dantzik	12	24
fo. 42 v.	49	Jan Hendrik Wilkes	Harrier (Starrier?)	12	24
	50	Andries Eekman	Lubeck	12	24
	51	Roelof de Wee	Amsterdam	12	24
	52	Jan Barendsz	Dantzik	12	24
	53	Christiaan Baakeij	Gottenburg	12	24
	54	Christoffel Tol	Wismer	12	24
fo. 43	55	Jan Keepers	Breemen	12	24
	56	Jan Jacobsz	Koningsbergen	12	24
	57	Jan Christoffel Rink	Berlijn	12	24
	58	Gerrit Jansz	Stapelmoe	12	24
	59	Christiaan Roelofz	Golno	12	24
	60	Carel Went	Dantzik	12	24
	61	Anderies Zwaan	Carelskroon	12	24

185

fo. 43 v.	62 Jan Godfried Grabien	Golno	12	24
	63 Jan Jacob Stokvliet	Dantzik	12	24
	64 Jan Fredrik Wiggers	Hamburg	12	24
	65 Pieter Valboom	Stokholm	12	24
	66 Hendrik de Meus	Amsterdam	12	24
	67 Jan Blank	Amsterdam	12	24
	68 Pieter Frederiksz	Laarkolen	12	24
	69 Adam Maas	Dantzig	12	24
fo. 44	70 Hans Douwesz	Lubeck	12	24
	71 Cornelis Kruytberg	Ahuyse	12	24
	72 Pieter Koldriaan	Dantzik	12	24
	73 Jacob Vos	Dantzik	12	24
	74 Harmen Davidsz	Leer	12	24
	75 Adrianus van Affen	Amsterdam	12	24
	76 Antony Eysing	Borghorst	12	24
	77 Anderies Legart	Straalzond	12	24
fo. 44 v.	78 Pieter Jelmers	Enkhuysen	12	24
	79 Hendrik Auriel	Hildesheim	12	24
	80 Foppe van Ewegen	Elens	12	24
	81 Hans Christoffel Hantz	Beien	12	24
	82 Jacob Berg	Carelskroon	12	24
	83 Jan Claasz	Amsterdam	12	24
	84 Hartman Wys	Dantzik	12	24
	85 Martin Fessener	Koningsbergen	12	24
	86 Gerrit Elsbeek	Amsterdam	12	24

fo. 45

BUSSCHIETERS *a f 11*
(Gun captains at 11 guilders a month)

	87 Dirk Myer	Deventer	11	22
	88 Pieter van Zweden	Rotterdam	11	22
	89 Johannes Keyzer	Amsterdam	11	22
	90 Jan Henderik Visser	Manshooft	11	22
	91 Tade Harmensz	Norden	11	22

fo. 45. v.	92 Jan Wijnverbeek	Amsterdam	11	22
	93 Jan Hendrik			
	Wilkes	Koekshaven	11	22
	94 Pieter Smit	Hamburg	11	22
	95 Andreas Pleuman	Calmer	11	22
fo. 46	96 Hendrik Tijssen	Amsterdam	11	22
	97 Engelke Kruijdop	Braak	11	22
	98 Jan Jacobsz	Abenrade	11	22
	99 Jan Frederik			
	Hersbergen	Sleeswijk	11	22
fo. 46 v.	100 Jochem Jacob			
	Golbeek	Straalsond	11	22
	101 Cornelis			
	Hendrikse	Duynkerke	11	22
	102 Hendrik Jansz	Rotterdam	11	22
	103 Jan Jacob de			
	Lange	Hamburg	11	22
fo. 47	blank			

fo. 48

BUSSCHIETERS *a f 10*
(Gun captains at 10 guilders a month)

	104 Willem Jansz			
	Kryt	Amsterdam	10	20
	105 Barend Dirksz	Amsterdam	10	20
	106 Leendert van der			
	Linden	Amsterdam	10	20
fo. 48 v.	107 Claas Pieteringh	Amsterdam	10	20
	108 Christiaen			
	Frederikse	Hoezem	10	20
	109 Henderik Kolee	Utrecht	10	20
	110 Ernst Lodewijk			
	Visser	Hanover	10	20
	111 Jan Jansz			
	Huijssloot	Hazerswouw	10	20
fo. 49	112 Pieter Hafham	Hamburgh	10	20
	113 Hermanus			
	Dideriks	Docerim	10	20
	114 Jonas Hammerlo	Calmer	10	20
	115 Jacob Middelvelt	Amsterdam	10	20
fo. 49 v.	116 Erik Johan Urner	Stokholm	10	20
	117 Pieter Jansze			
	Roele	Crommeniedijk	10	20

	118	Luycas Drinkveldt	Bergen op Zoom	10	20
	119	Melchior Tyssen	Eykervliet	10	20
fo. 50	120	Marten Kieft	Amsterdam	10	20
	121	Cornelis Nellissen	Saarse	10	20
	122	Jan Sybrandt	Litter	10	20
	123	Arend Graverts	Amsterdam	10	20
	124	Jan Dirksz	Holstyn	10	20
	125	Pieter Pietersz	Langeland	10	20
	126	Fredrik Carel Bassenberg	Riscking	10	20
	127	Jacob Schulte	Straalsond	10	20

MATROOSEN *a f 9*
(Ordinary seamen at 9 guilders a month)

	128	Jan Jochem Beemt	Hamburg	9	18
	129	Jan de Roos	Campen	9	18
	130	Jurgen Peesen	Amsterdam	9	18
	131	Claas van Diersen	Ditmarsen	9	18
fo. 51	132	Hendrik Wieriks	Sneek	9	18
	133	Heyn Ojers	Hoorn	9	18
	134	Johannes Ellek	Zweeden	9	18
	135	Jan Smit	Amsterdam	9	18
fo. 51 v.	136	Jan Francois	Amsterdam	9	18
	137	Mattheys Hank	Flensburgh	9	18
	138	Ariaen Teunisze	Liste	9	18
fo. 52	139	Christiaen Christiaensz Huyer	Flensburg	9	18
	140	Salemon Margenout	Ceylon	9	18
	141	Arnoldus de Bonne	Ceylon	9	18
	142	Jacob Eysendoorn	Utrecht	9	18
fo. 52 v.	143	Hendrik Christoffel Breslers	Milhousen	9	18
	144	Dirk Jansz de Groot	d'Ryp	9	18
	145	Gustavus Cullijn	Waasbergen	9	18

fo. 53

JONG-MATROOSEN *a f 8*
(Young seamen at 8 guilders a month)

146	Jan Jacob Pelte	Amsterdam	8	16
147	Booy Jansen	Veur	8	16
148	Dirk Dirksen	Amsterdam	8	16
149	Albert Nicolaas Dornhek	Amsterdam	8	16
fo. 53 v. 150	Dirk Pieterz	Crommenie	8	16
151	Matthias Laurens August Bandauw	Altena	8	16
152	Nicolaas Christiaansz	Flensburg	8	16
153	Jan Aalders	Amsterdam	8	16
fo. 54 154	Jan Carstens	Amsterdam	8	16
155	Jan Udeman	Amsterdam	8	16
156	Frans Gijzelingh	Amsterdam	8	16
157	Jannes Scheefers	Paterborn	8	16
158	Jan La Mot	Ceylon	8	16
fo. 54 v. 159	Hendrik Hendriksz	Ceylon	8	16
160	Abram Kamerling	Amsterdam	8	16
161	Willem Tjerk	Amsterdam	8	16
162	Jan Draij	Amsterdam	8	16
163	Gerrit Brand	De Haag	8	16
164	Cornelis Sieket	Ceylon	8	16
165	Jacob Brevoet	Zwol	8	16

fo. 55

HOOPLOPERS *a f 7*
(Apprentice seaman at 7 guilders a month)

166	Harmanus Hartgers	Amsterdam	7	14
167	Henderik Fontein	Leijden	7	14
168	Frans Lelienberg	Amsterdam	7	14
169	Willem Dokter	Amsterdam	7	14
fo. 55 v. 170	Simon Wydekamp	Amsterdam	7	14
171	Pieter Gerritz	Amsterdam	7	14
172	Hendrik Wyngaarde	Amsterdam	7	14

	173	Jan van Laar	Amsterdam		7	14
	174	Pieter van Dieveren	Amsterdam		7	14
fo. 56	175	Stoffel Roelofz	Coppenhagen		7	14
	176	Daniel de Gansch	Amsterdam		7	14
	177	Jan Stapel	Amsterdam		7	14
	178	Jan Axtholm	Amsterdam		7	14
	179	Gerrit de Grijs	Amsterdam		7	14
fo. 56 v.	180	Simon van der Wouden	Amsterdam		7	14
	181	Jacobus de Haan	Amsterdam		7	14
	182	Dirk Jansz van Leeuwen	Amsterdam		7	14
	183	Jan van Heusden	Amsterdam		7	14
	184	Antonie Onsle	Amsterdam		7	14
fo. 57	185	Johannes Krooneman	Amsterdam		7	14
	186	Pieter de Graaf	Amsterdam		7	14
	187	Jan Bosschaert	Amsterdam		7	14
	188	Jacob Baks	Allendorff		7	14

fo. 58

JONGENS *a f 5*

(Ship's boys, under 16 years old, at 5 guilders)

	189	Adrianus Welgevaren	Leerdam		5	10
	190	Dirk Raademaker	Amsterdam		5	10
	191	Dirk de Maree	Gouda		5	10

fo. 59

AMBAGTS–LIEDEN

(Craftsmen and artisans)

	192	Gerrit Kok	Aarnhem	Timmerman (Carpenter)	15	30
	193	Johan Dirk Ronged	Delmenhorst	Grofsmit (Smith)	14	28
	194	Jacobus Martensz	Amsterdam	Roerslotemaker (Locksmith)	14	28
fo. 59 v.	195	Nicolaas van Beusekom	Utrecht	Huys Timmerman (House carpenter)	12	24
	196	Dirk van Munster	Utrecht	Metzelaar (Mason)	14	28
	197	Jochem Rymer	Kerlin	Grofsmit (Smith)	14	28

	198	Jurgen Ollenbuttel	Scharpen-stoetel	Grofsmit (Smith)	14	28
fo. 60	199	Jan Hendrik Steinbekker	Aalen	Grofsmit (Smith)	14	28
	200	Jacobus Kramer	Amsterdam	Metzelaar (Mason)	14	28
	201	Cornelis Slimwint	Ouwedelie	Roerslotemaker (Locksmith)	14	28
	202	Johan Mechiel Hetsel	Rommers-wyle	Wagemaker (Cartwright)	14	28
fo. 60 v.	203	Jacob Hal	Amsterdam	Luijtenant Militair (Military Lieutenant)	50	100

fo. 61   MILITAIRE OFFICIEREN
                           (Military Officers)

	204	Gerard van Hoeij	's Graven-hage	Sergeant (Sergeant)	20	40
	205	Frederik August Sparman	Dresden	Corporael (Corporal)	14	28
	206	Johan David Bestholst	Mitweede	Corporael (Corporal)	14	28
	207	Johannis Sluijters	Amsterdam	Tamboer (Drummer)	9	18

fo. 61 v.   SOLDAATEN
                            (Soldiers)
              allen per maand 9 dus per 2 maanden
        (All paid 9 guilders a month, two months in advance)

	208	Philip Coster	Rijssel
fo. 62	209	Lucas Hoers	Engelstad
	210	Johan Christoffel Michael Muller	Hessen
	211	Henry Toussin	Navarre
	212	Godhart Johan Jordaan	Riga
	213	Thomas Ronske	Koningsbergen

fo. 63	214	Antoon Ringemoet	Huij
	215	Johan Daniel Haake	Braakwe
	216	Gerrit Willem Speelingh	Meppelt
	217	Jan Harme Janneman	Munster
fo. 63 v.	218	Maximiliaen Brand	Waldek
	219	Christiaan Schaats	Reedenouw
	220	Hendrik Schryvers	Langevelt
	221	Jan Lodewijk Rosler	Neuburg
fo. 64	222	Thomas Hellings	Amsterdam
	223	Dirk Drouwé	Amsterdam
	224	Carol Foks	Neurenbergh
	225	Joseph Klinkert	Ceulstourland
fo. 64 v.	226	Carel Rosijn	Zutphen
	227	Johan Daniel Heijmas	Steekenroode
	228	Frans Joseph Witmeijer	Roodenburg
fo. 65	229	Jan Casper Erwigh	Wezel
	230	Pieter Spierling	Amsterdam
	231	Joost Cammeijer	Westhelver
	232	Gregorius Stensel (destination Cape)	Steyr
	233	Coert Henderik Ditmaring	Hanover
fo. 65 v.	234	Johann Christoffel Anholt	Dresden
	235	Jan Hendrik Fik	Wismer
	236	Alexander Coster	Mekkelenbergh
	237	Jan de Ruijter	Cappel
	238	Dedelof Pietersz	Hamburgh
fo. 66	239	Henderik Caaneman	Beurer
	240	Andreas Coert	Anhalt Grote

	241	Coenraad Ernst Sinxsstaagh	Hamburg
	242	Gregorius Stentzel	Breslouw
	243	Carel Alme	Zurigh
fo. 66 v.	244	Jan van Wiggelink-huijzen	Amersfoort
	245	Johan George Coenraad Raan	Berdewil
	246	Dedelof Arendts	Holsteyn
	247	Balthazar Kleiger	Italie
	248	Jens Thomasz	Werdel
fo. 67	249	Johannis Eeke	Nuijs
	250	Johannis Stoklenbergh	Oostenrijk
	251	Jan Herman Menge	Munsterland
	252	Henderik Oostenbrugge	Hamburgh
	253	Henderik Jobs	Maanen
fo. 67 v.	254	David Rohr	Coningsbergen
	255	Rinke Teunis (destination Cape)	Doccum
	256	Casper van Salingen	Anhalt
	257	Jacob Ernst Blinkner	Belzen
	258	Gasper Elcar	Dantzig
fo. 68 v.	259	Jochem Knol	Lubeck
	260	Ernst Eekhout	Mekelenburg
	261	Hans Lodewig Gons (destination Cape)	Swabeland
	262	Christiaan Notjes	Hanover
	263	Pieter Gerard	Pomeren
fo. 68 v.	264	Frederik Laske	Coningsbergen
	265	Christiaen Frederik Reezeler	Ter Walder

	266	Michiel Groen	Elbink
	267	Christiaen Herrenbosch	Hanover
fo. 69	269	Christoffel Reijtz	Lodewijksburgh
	270	Robbert Toelers	St. Pieters-Visnaakx
	271	Michiel Schiphols	Swaaby
	272	Johan Christiaen Reijts	Marrienburgh
	273	Jacob Beerens	Hamburgh
	274	Adrianus Droogh	Amsterdam
	275	Henderik Jacob Schreuders	't Cluyst Limberg
	276	Johannis Jooste	Nassau-Dillenburgh
	277	Michiel Leonsi	Menningen
	278	Jan Coppel	Wesel
fo. 69 v.	279	Samuel Smook	Eijtien
	280	Johannes Diderik	Hessencassel
	281	Robertus Seines	Erfurt
	282	Meink Jansz	Aurick
	283	Jan Christiaen Henderik Baarmeester	Oldenburgh
	284	Hans Seijtenoff	Hildesheijm
	285	Jan Joost Wolf	Landouw
	286	Barend Rugers (destination Cape)	Meppelt
	287	Anthoon Sixfransz	Sittouw
	288	Samuel Pieterman	Sittouw
fo. 70	289	Jan Diderigh Berendt	Hanover
	290	Hans Jacob Slivert	Elzas
	291	Jacob Jens	Bazel
	292	Lodewijk Frederik Wagener (destination Cape)	Wurtembergh

	293 Frans Spinkelingh (destination Cape)	Rietsing
	294 Albert Geubels	Soest
	295 Jean Joseph	Schafhauzen
	296 David Ferdinandus Seijmer	Wien
	297 Hans Jurge Carstingh	Hamburgh
	298 Jan Henderik Anschuts	Erfort
fo. 70 v.	299 Jacob Adam Kok	Frankenhauzen
	300 Coenraad Biebert	Gilhauzen
	301 Dirk Nonna	Utrecht
	302 Jan de Let	Naamen
	303 Samuel Schertelingh	Eysleeben
	304 Jacob Teer	Radstad
	305 Johan Godfried Schoonman	Cylemburg
	306 Henderik Gelder	Zwabelandt
	307 Pieter Millenas	Bon
	308 Jan Frederik Gieler	Altmarkt
fo. 71	309 Harme Waterman	Sinhorst
	310 Johan Frederik Baartscheerder	Berlin
	311 Class Weijs	Zurigh
	312 Jacob Lodewijk Rudolff Wilhelmi	Bronswijk
	313 Nicholaas Koningh	Coningsbergen
	314 Frederik Grabo	Broesen
	315 Dirk Bestenhorst	Amsterdam
	316 Wander Armbrost	Hoksbergen
	317 Johan Samuel Tierens	Pruijssen
	318 Arend Willekes	Oldenburgh
	319 Gerardus Theodorus Pot	Essen

fo. 71 v.	320	Henderik Spangert	Weerdel
	321	Hartman Smitz	Canton Bern
	322	Casper Belke	Hespelhuijzerwinkel
	323	Henderik Jurge Coorts	Bronswijk
	324	Benedictus Leo	Jurgouw
	325	Augustinus Mulder	Amsterdam
	326	Andreas Quinte	Greevensteijn
	327	Anthonij Kempenaer	Hamburg
	328	Engel Gabriel	Haarlem
fo. 72	329	Jan Harme Weezeman	Breemen
	330	Jan Henderik Boode	Bronswijk

APPENDIX C

Select Bibliography and Sources

The Dutch East India Company

C. R. Boxer, *The Dutch Seaborne Empire 1600–1800*, Hutchinson, London, 1965.

C. R. Boxer, 'The Dutch East Indiamen: their Sailors, their Navigators, and Life on Board, 1602–1795', *Mariner's Mirror* (1963), vol. 49, pp. 81–104. These are both extremely important general works on the VOC, and have extensive footnotes and references to many other publications dealing with the Company.

B.B.C. publication, *Europe and the Indies: the Era of the Companies, 1600–1824*, London, 1970.

K. Glamann, *Dutch-Asiatic Trade, 1620–1740*, Copenhagen and The Hague, 1958.

J. S. Stavorinus, *Voyages to the Cape of Good Hope, Batavia, etc.* (1768), published in English translation from the Dutch in 1798. There is a copy in the National Maritime Museum, Greenwich.

Instructie ten dienste van de lading der schepen in Oost-Indie, published about 1689 for the VOC. This describes the loading of extra quantities of cargo in VOC ships.

'An exact account of the rise, progress, and present state of the Dutch East-India Company', in *Lloyds Evening Post*, London, July–December 1757, pp. 525, 526, 533.

Building and Equipping the Amsterdam

'Resolutions of the Heeren XVII', *Kol. Arch.* 274, 3 August 1747, 2 April 1748, 14 September 1748, 19 November 1748.

'Journalen van de Opperboek houder der Kamer Amsterdam', *Kol. Arch.* 10429, pp. 39, 80. 114, 163, 289, 315.

K. M. C. Zevenboom, *Amstelodamum*, 1953.

'Resolution of the Amsterdam Chamber', *Kol. Arch.* 392, 3 October 1748.

Debts of Klump, van Bockom, and van Hoeij

Municipal Archives of Amsterdam:

W. Klump, *Not. Arch.* inv. nos. 10924, 10925.

G. van Hoeij, *Not. Arch.* inv. no. 12172, acts nos. 461, 462.

A. van Bockom, *Not. Arch.* inv. no. 11544, acts nos. 26, 27, 28.

Also, 'Payroll of the departing Fair, Christmas, and Easter ships, 1748–9', at the Algemeen Rijksarchief, *Kol. Arch.* inv. no. 9549.

The Voyage

'Uitloopboek voor schepen 1688–1803', *Kol. Arch.* 43900–A, p. 61.

Amsterdamse Donderdaegse Courant, 2 November 1748 (no. 140); 6 February 1749 (no. 16).

Amsterdamse Dingsdaegse Courant, 10 December 1748 (no. 148); 28 January 1749 (no. 12); 4 February 1749 (no. 15).

Amsterdamse Saturdaegse Courant, 1 February 1749 (no. 14).

Nederlandsch Gedenkboek of Europische Mercurius, January 1749, pp. 78–9; February 1749, pp. 122, 123.

Dutch Records of the Shipwreck

Resolutions of the Amsterdam Chamber:
> *Kol. Arch.* 392, 10 February 1749, 20 February 1749, 24 February 1749, 27 February 1749, 6 March 1749, 11 March 1749, 3 April 1749, 4 April 1749, 21 April 1749, 8 May 1749, 19 May 1749.
> *Kol. Arch.* 393, 21 May 1750, 1 June 1750.

Resolutions of the Heeren XVII:
> *Kol. Arch.* 275, 5 March 1749, 14 April 1749.

'Journalen van de Opperboekhouder van der Amsterdamse Kamer', *Kol. Arch.* 10429, p. 206; p. 268 (31 May 1749); p. 315 (27 June 1749); p. 320 (30 June 1749); p. 368 (30 September 1749); also entries for 15 May 1750 and 28 February 1751.

English Records of the Shipwreck

C. L. Sayer (editor), *The correspondence of Mr John Collier, and his family, 1716–80*, London, 1907, vol. 1.

Biography of John Collier in *Sussex Archaeological Collections*, vol. XLV (1902), p. 62.

The 'Collier Letters' at East Sussex Record Office, Lewes:
> Letter from Thomas Smith, dated 17 January 1748 (Old Style date).
> Letter from Mrs Smith, dated 17 January 1748 (OS).
> Letter from George Worge, dated 17 January 1748 (OS).
> Letter from Richard Patrick, dated 24 January 1748 (OS).
> Letter from Richard Patrick, dated 31 January 1748 (OS).
> Letter from Dr Russell, dated 6 February 1748 (OS).
> Letter from George Worge, dated 11 February 1748 (OS).
> Letter from Mr Thorpe, dated 22 February 1748 (OS).

There is an extract from a contemporary newspaper of 1748–9, not named, which is quoted in *Brett's Gazette*, file in Hastings Reference Library.

Sussex Smugglers

The Gentleman's Magazine, 1748, vol. XVIII, pp. 407, 425, 475, 572.

The Gentleman's Magazine, 1749, vol. XIX, pp. 28, 29, 30, 42, 43.

The account of the wreck of the *Nympha Americana* appears in *The Sussex County Magazine*, 1927, vol. 1, p. 212; and the original oil painting depicting the wreck is in Lewes Museum.

The play *The Shipwreck* by William Hyland was reprinted in *The Sussex County Magazine*, 1927, vol. 1, p. 219.

Weather conditions

The weather conditions of winter 1748–9 given in this book are based on a general weather report for January 1749 preserved by the Meteorological Office; on newspaper reports of the period in the Burney Collection in the British Museum, especially those of *The Penny London Post* and *The General Advertiser*; and on a report in *The Gentleman's Magazine*, 1749, p. 43.

Hastings history and geology

'The Wealden district', British regional geology, 1954, published by HMSO.

Geological Survey Map, sheet 320, published by HMSO.

J. Manwaring Baines, *Historic Hastings*, Hastings, 1955.

W. D. Parish, *A Dictionary of the Sussex dialect*, Lewes, 1875.

H. B. Milner and A. J. Bull, 'Geology of the Eastbourne – Hastings coastline', *Proceedings of the Geological Association*, vol. XXXVI (1925), pp. 304, 317.

Later references to the Amsterdam *and its site*

Many of these references to the *Amsterdam* are very inaccurate and must be used with caution. Most of them can be found in Hastings Reference Library. Some I have not been able to check and are quoted in the MS of J. Lucus *Book of Amsterdam*, 1911, which is preserved in Hastings Library.

The Gentleman's Magazine, 1786, pt. 2, pp. 649–51, 852–4.

The Antiquarian and Topographical Cabinet, 1808, vol. 4, Bulverhithe.

T. B. Brett's *Diary* under date of 10 February 1827.

Henry Phillips of Hastings, *Diaries 1825–29*; entries under 12, 14 February 1827. East Sussex Record Office, Ams. 5788/2/3.

R. L. Jones, *The Latest Edition of the Hastings Guide*, Hastings, 1827, p. 56.

Annual Register, 1827, 'Chronicle', p. 35.

I. D. Parry, *An historical and descriptive account of the coast of Sussex*, London, 1833, p. 241

Woll's *Strangers' Guide to Hastings & St Leonards*, Hastings, 1833?, p. 50.

T. W. Horsfield, *The history, antiquities, and topography of the county of Sussex*, London, 1835, vol. 1, p. 431.
Southall's pocket Guide to St Leonards and Hastings, 1st ed., 1835, 5th ed., p. 58.
Ross's Hastings and St Leonards Guide, Hastings, 1835, p. 49.
A. Cross, *A ramble about Hastings and St Leonards, and their neighbourhood*, Hastings, 1848, chapter X, p. 53.
I. Hope, *Hope's pictorial guide to Hastings and St Leonards*, Hastings, c. 1849, p. 43.
Osborne's *Strangers' Guide*, 1853, p. 69.
M. Howard, *A Handbook for Hastings and St Leonards*, Hastings, 1855, 3rd edition 1864, p. 122.
J. Dorman, *A Guide to St Leonards-on-Sea & Hastings*, St Leonards-on-Sea, 1867, p. 57.
Brett's *St Leonards Gazette*, 31 August 1878, 12 April 1879, 1 May 1880, filed in *Premier Cinque Port*, vol. 1, pp. 87–8.
N. May, *Guide to Hastings and St Leonards*, London, 1884, p. 78.
Pictorial and descriptive guide to Hastings, St Leonards, Bexhill, etc., Ward Lock & Co., London, 2nd ed. 1898–9?, p. 95.
Parson's guide to Hastings and St Leonards, Hastings, p. 144.
P. M. Powell, *Hastings Guide*, 5th ed., p. 64.

Ships

J. R. Stevens, *An Account of the construction, and embellishment, of old time ships*, privately printed, Toronto, 1949.
H. Ketting, Prins Willem: *een zeventiende eeuwse Oostindievaarder, Bussum, 1979*, is a superb study of a 17th century East Indiaman.

There are some drawings of Dutch East Indiamen in the Prins Hendrik Maritime Museum, Rotterdam, and in the Scheepvaart Museum, Amsterdam. These ships are often depicted in paintings and engravings which can also be found at the Rijksmuseum, Amsterdam.

A number of fine models of Dutch East Indiamen also exist, or existed until recently, which bear the following names:
Valkenisse, 1717, Museum of Fine Arts, Boston, U.S.A.
Bataviase Eeuw, 1719, Royal Scottish Museum, Edinburgh.
Gertruda, 1720, Scheepvaart, Museum, Amsterdam.
Principe da Bera(?), Lisbon (destroyed).
Padmos–Blydorp, Prins Hendrik Museum, Rotterdam.
Zevene Provincien, 1723, National Maritime Museum, Greenwich.
Ary, 1725 at the Scheepvaart Museum, Amsterdam.
A most important Dutch East Indiaman for study of the *Amsterdam* is the

Mercurius of 58 guns, built 1747, which is preserved in the Rijksmuseum, Amsterdam.

See. R. C. Anderson, 'Models of Dutch East Indiamen, 1716–1725', *Mariner's Mirror*, 1932, vol. 18, pp. 161–7; 1933, vol. 19, pp. 343–4; 1935, vol. 21, p. 206.

Wrecks of Dutch East Indiamen

Archaeological information about VOC shipwrecks is being published, but there is still an urgent need for full publication in such international media as the *International Journal of Nautical Archaeology*, published by the Council for Nautical Archaeology, Institute of Archaeology, 31–4 Gordon Square, London, WC1.

Australia

Batavia (1629): *History Today*, 1972, vol. 22, no. 10, pp. 706–15; P. Tyler, 'The *Batavia* Mutineers', *Westerly* (pub. in Western Australia), December 1970, no. 4, pp. 32–45. Information on this and other Australian wrecks is also contained in Henrietta Drake-Brockman, *Voyage to Disaster* (1963), Sydney, Australia; Hugh Edwards, *Wreck on the Half Moon Reef* (Robert Hale, 1970) and Hugh Edwards, *Islands of Angry Ghosts* (Hodder/Angus & Robertson, 1969).

Vergulde Draeck (1656): J. N. Green, 'The Wreck of the Dutch East Indiaman the *Vergulde Draeck*, 1656', *International Journal of Nautical Archaeology*, 1973, vol. 2, no. 2, pp. 267–89, and J. N. Green (ed.), *The A-VOC Jacht* Vergulde Draeck, *wrecked Western Australia, 1656*, parts I and II, BAR Supplementary Series 36, 1977. See also C. R. Boxer, 'Plata es Sangre: sidelights on the drain of Spanish-American silver in the Far East, 1550–1700', *Philippine Studies*, 1970, vol. 18, no. 3.

Zeewijk (1727): C. Ingelman-Sundberg, *Relics from the Dutch East Indiaman Zeewijk*. Western Australian Museum Special Publication, no. 10, 1978.

Britain

Lastdrager (1653): Sotheby's auction catalogue, *Treasure recovered off the Shetland Isles*, for 8 November 1973; C. R. Boxer, 'Treasure from the sea: Shipwrecks of Dutch East Indiamen 1629–1749', *History Today*, 1973, vol. xxiii, no. 11, pp. 766–75.

Kennemerland (1664): *The Observer* colour supplement, 14 November 1971; W. Forster and K. Higgs, 'The *Kennemerland*, an interim report', in *International Journal of Nautical Archaeology*, 1973, vol. 2, no. 2, pp. 291–300.

de Liefde (1711): A. Bax and C. Martin, '*De Liefde*, a Dutch East Indiaman lost on the Out Skerries, Shetland', in *International Journal of Nautical Archaeology*, 1974, vol. 3, pp. 81–90.

Hollandia (1743): *Daily Telegraph Magazine*, no. 387, 29 March 1972; C. R. Boxer, 'The *Hollandia* treasure and its historical significance' in Sotheby's auction catalogue *Hollandia Coins and other artefacts* for 18 April 1972; W. H. Lane & Sons, Penzance, auction *Catalogue of coins, etc., from the 'Hollandia'*, for 8 September 1972.

Netherlands

T Vliegend Hart (1735): J. Gawronski and B. Kist, T Vliegend Hart *Report 1982–3*, Rijksmuseum, Amsterdam, 1984.

St Helena

Witte Leeuw (1613): C. L. vasn der Pijl-Ketel and J. B. Kist, *The Ceramic Load of the* Witte Leeuw, *1613*, Rijksmuseum, Amsterdam, 1982.

South Africa

Merestijn (1702) and *Middelburg* (1781): John Marcus & Sons, 98 Long Street, Cape Town, South Africa, auction catalogue for 21 January 1972. For the *Merestijn*, see P. Marsden, 'The *Merestijn*, wrecked in 1702, near Cape Town, South Africa,' in *International Journal of Nautical Archaeology*, 1976, vol. 5, pp. 201–19.

? *Nieuw Rhoon* (1776): R. A. Lightley, 'An 18th Century Dutch East Indiaman, found near Cape Town, 1971,' in *International Journal of Nautical Archaeology*, 1976, vol. 5, pp. 305–16.

Antiquities

Ivor Noël Hume, *A Guide to the artefacts of Colonial America*, Knopf, New York, 1970.

G. Bass (editor), *A History of Seafaring, based on Underwater Archaeology*, Thames & Hudson, 1972. See especially M. Peterson, 'Traders and Privateers across the Atlantic: 1493–1733', pp. 253–80, for details of the Spanish movement of treasure prior to its use by the Dutch East India Company.

Opgravingen in Amsterdam, Amsterdam Historisch Museum Afdeling Archaeologie, Amsterdam, 1977.

Submarine archaeological investigation

Surveying in archaeology underwater, Colt Archaeological Institute, Monograph series 5, 1969. See especially E. T. Hall, 'Electronic instruments in underwater surveys', pp. 21–31, which describes the use of proton magnetometers and metal detectors.

D. Blackman (editor), *Marine Archaeology*, Colston Research Society, 1973. See especially A. McKee, 'The Search for King Henry VIII's *Mary Rose*', pp. 185–98.

D. Rosencrantz, M. Klein, H. Egerton, 'The uses of sonar', in *Underwater Archaeology, a nascent discipline*, pp. 257–70, UNESCO publication, Paris, 1972.

E. T. Hall, 'Wreck prospecting by magnetometer', in *Underwater Archaeology, a nascent discipline*, pp. 285–93, UNESCO publication, Paris, 1972.

Raising and preserving ships

B. Brorson Christensen, *The Conservation of waterlogged wood in the National Museum of Denmark*, Copenhagen, 1970.

Conservation of Waterlogged Wood, UNESCO and the 'Save the Amsterdam Foundation', The Hague, 1981.

Lars Barkman, *On resurrecting a wreck*, Statens Sjöhistoriska Museum, Stockholm, 1967.

Anders Franzén, *The Warship Vasa*, Stockholm, 1966.

Index

Aalders, Jan, 40, 138, 139 (spoon, fig 25), 189

Aaron, Jack, 90, 92

Adams, Jon, 106, 152, 164

Amsterdam, construction 22–3, 27 (pl II), 197, 113 (tumble-home), 197; contents, *passim* and 86–94, 121–39 (figs 11–25); payroll, 27 (pl II), 28–9, 179–96; maiden voyage 38–46, 39 (course, fig 3), 46 (mutiny), 48 (beached), 181, 198; accounts of the wreck, see under Collier letters, and later accounts 82–5

salvage: [1749] 60–1, 64–73, 83, 174–8; [1810] 83–4, 86; [1827] 86, 88; [1837] 88; [1937 confidence trick] 90; [1969] 90–95, 165 (mechanical excavator at work, pl XXII)

archaeological excavation: [1969] 103–19, 107 (overall view of site, pl XII); probed profiles, 97 (position, fig 5), 116 (fig 8), 118; plan and side elevation *in situ*, 106 (fig 6); magnetometer survey, 117 (fig 9); metal detector survey and aerial view, 105 (pl XI), excavation of port side, 111 (fig 7); recording starboard, lower deck supports and port side excavation, 141 (pl XIV); [1984] 147–63, diving platform, (col pl between pp 72–73), sketch of excavated stern, 165 (pl XXII); timber base of officer's toilets, 149 (pl XV), 159; fishtail decoration, 159, 161 (pl XXI); possible survival of figurehead, 170; future plans 164–71; outline reconstruction in section, 97 (fig 5); possibility of eventual accurate reconstruction, 166–71; significance of ship, 171–3

See also under: armament, barrels, book, brushes, candlesticks, clay pipes, cutlery, dress, glass, irons, pottery, pulley blocks, surgeon's equipment, tobacco box

Amsterdam, City of, 18–19 (map, fig 1), 147; coat of arms, 170; Central Laboratory, 152, 160, 162; municipal records, 26; Rijksmuseum, 159, 166; Scheepvaart Museum, 144, 166; Stork Werkspoor private museum, 171

Amsterdam Foundation, Save the, 147, 162

Amsterdam Thursday Journal, 64

armament: bronze cannon, 93, (col pl between pp 72–73), 124–5 (figs 14 and 15), gunport 109 (pl XIII), 110; musket balls, 49 (pl V), cartridge belt, 93, 136 (fig 23); sword belt, 135 (fig 22)

Australia, 120 (fig 10), 201

Baines, John Manwaring, 62, 90, 99, 102, 119

Barrie, Peter, 152

barrels: 91, 92, (col pl between pp 72–73), 89 (pl IX), 123 (fig 13), 158 (fig 27)

GET ON FIRST NAME TERMS with some of the WORLD'S MOST AMAZING PEOPLE!

Technological powerhouse and innovator

Feisty women's-rights campaigner

High-flying feminist icon

Death-defying escape artist

Teenage activist for girls' rights

The woman who made coding cool

The man who abolished slavery in the US

Gifted, globetrotting Portuguese pioneer

The most intelligent man who ever lived?

Superwoman and superstar

World-famous freedom fighter